SCHOOL LAW CASEBOOK SERIES—NO. 2

The Law Relating to the Creation, Alteration, and Dissolution of School Districts

By
LEE O. GARBER
and
NEWTON EDWARDS

The Interstate
Printers and Publishers
Danville, Illinois

Library of Congress
Catalog Card Number: 62-19686

CONTENTS

INTRODUCTION

This book is the second in a series of proposed casebooks which, taken together, will give complete coverage to the field of school law. The same general plan followed in the first book is followed here. It includes a brief statement of legal principles underlying the topic under discussion, followed by excerpts chosen from leading cases selected to provide concrete illustrations of the important principles mentioned. Other books covering other aspects of school law will be published in this series.

The authors are well known for their contributions to the field of "School Law." Newton Edwards, Professor Emeritus, University of Chicago, has written numerous articles and is author of the well-known leading text in this field—*The Courts and the Public Schools.* Lee O. Garber, Professor of Education, University of Pennsylvania, has prepared the *Yearbook of School Law* annually since 1950. In addition, he is known for his articles of timely interest which have been a regular feature of *The Nation's Schools* for the last decade.

Russell L. Guin,
Publisher

Authors' Preface

In the preparation of this series of casebooks in "School Law" the authors are achieving an ambition of long standing. For some time they have felt the need of a casebook or books to supplement the textbooks available in this field. Every student of school law should acquaint himself with material from the original sources—the court decisions themselves. This is essential if one is to understand the reasoning the courts employ as they arrive at their decisions, as well as the legal principles underlying them. Because many students of "School Law" do not have access to law libraries, it is particularly important that they have the case material available for their use.

In addition, a number of universities engaged in the preparation of teachers and administrators integrate school law with other courses rather than teach it as a special subject. Where such is the practice, this series of casebooks should be of special value. The authors hope that this book may also prove of value in supplementing units of work in such courses as "Introduction to Education" and "Personnel Administration."

A word about the organization of this book is important. It will be noted that it has two main parts. Part I is devoted to a discussion of significant legal principles. Part II consists of the court decisions themselves. It will also be noted that introducing each case is a quotation taken from the section on "Legal Principles." Following each case is a series of questions, "Guides for Class Discussion." These are only suggestive and are not intended to be comprehensive. It is hoped, however, that they will serve to focus attention upon the essential principles.

The reader should be warned that the "Legal Principles" are of a general nature. They are those generally accepted by the courts in the absence of controlling statutes. With respect to almost every legal principle it may be said that in some jurisdictions the courts have taken a different point of view. Consequently, in reading this material one should keep in mind any exceptions which the courts of his particular state may have adopted.

Lee O. Garber
Newton Edwards

I.

LEGAL PRINCIPLES

Legal Principles

Authority over education vests in the state, but in order to carry out its policies the state finds it expedient to create local administrative units. Upon these administrative units the state confers certain powers and duties. The local administrative unit for education is commonly known as a school district, and its officers are designated the school board or the board of education.

The State and the Creation of School Districts

The state, acting through the legislature, may create whatever type of local school administrative organization it may desire. It may designate as school districts such civil divisions of the state as towns, cities, townships, or counties. If it seems the better policy, districts may be created which have no territorial relationship to existing civil divisions of the state.

School Districts Are Quasi-Corporations

The local school corporation, whatever type it may be, is a quasi-corporation, or a quasi-municipal corporation, as distinguished from a municipal corporation proper. A quasi-corporation is an agency of the state, created for the purpose of carrying into effect policies of state-wide concern. Its territory may be identical with that of a municipal corporation proper, but its functions are never essentially local. The quasi-corporation is concerned with the execution of state and not local policy. On the other hand, municipal corporations proper, such as towns and cities, are not primarily instruments of state policy; they are created to enable local communities to regulate and administer their own peculiar local concerns.

Method of Creating School Districts

The state is unrestricted in its choice of method of establishing school districts. It may establish them by direct legislative enactment, it may delegate its authority to establish districts to some administrative board or official, or it may make the creation of a district contingent upon the consent of the inhabitants affected. Since education is essentially a matter of state concern, school districts may be created with or without the consent of those who live in them.

Delegation of Authority to Create

When the state makes use of some administrative board or official in the establishment of school districts, care must be taken not to confer upon such board or official legislative authority. The legislature may delegate administrative authority but it may not delegate legislative authority. Such authority the legislature must exercise itself. Where an administrative agency is authorized to create school districts with no significant limitation upon its discretion, it is authorized to execute legislative powers and its acts will generally be declared void. Where, on the other hand, the legislature restricts the discretion of the administrative agency by requiring it to act within the limits of designated policies or standards, the authority exercised is administrative and will be sustained by the courts, as long as it conforms to the statute. In this connection it should be noted that with the creation of such districts, the courts have no concern; and they will not review an administrative agency's action in creating a district, in the absence of statute giving them that authority, unless it can be shown that the agency acted in a fraudulent, arbitrary, or unreasonable manner.

Elections for Approving the Creation of School Districts

The provisions of a statute providing for the establishment of school districts with the consent of the residents of the territory affected must be strictly followed. If a petition is required for the calling of an election to determine the will of the inhabitants, the filing of the petition is jurisdictional, and any election held without the required petition having been filed is void. Anyone who signs a petition may withdraw his name from it at any time before action has been taken by those to whom the petition is addressed, so it is generally held. Statutory provisions with respect to the giving of notice of an election are mandatory and must be substantially followed or the election will be void. But in all matters involved in the establishment of school districts, such as the giving of notice of an election, the posting of notices and the description of boundaries, substantial rather than technical compliance with the statute is all that is necessary. The courts will not permit minor irregularities, which could not have affected the outcome of an election, to defeat the will of the people. This is particularly true where the irregularity is complained of after the election has been held. As a result courts have generally accepted the rule that statutory provisions will be treated as mandatory before an election, but as directory afterwards.

Abolition and Alteration of School Districts

Since school districts are but parts of the machinery employed in carrying out the educational policies of the state, the legislature, in addition to creating school districts, may abolish them, or alter their boundaries as public policy may dictate. When district boundaries are changed, the legislature may dispose of property and of pre-existing assets and liabilities in such manner as may be deemed reasonable and just. School districts have no vested rights in school property because school property is state property merely held in trust for the state by the local authorities. Moreover, the transfer of property from one district to another is not a violation of rights guaranteed by the federal constitution. Such transfer of property is not in violation of a contract because no contractual relation exists between the state and its school districts. Nor does the transfer of property from district to district by annexation of territory violate the due-process-of-law clause of the Fourteenth Amendment.

Apportionment of Assets and Liabilities of Altered Districts

In case there is no statute governing the disposition of property or the apportionment of debts upon the alteration of district boundaries, the general rule adopted by the courts is that the property belongs to the district in which it is finally located and each district is liable for the debts it contracted before the change.

Where a district goes out of existence by annexation to another district or merges with other districts, the rule is that the subsisting district is entitled to the property and funds and answerable for the debts of the original corporation. In the absence of a statute governing the situation, funds in the possession of a district from which territory is detached continue to belong to the district.

De Facto Districts

School districts which have been illegally created may, nevertheless, function for some time as though they were legal. Whether or not their acts are legally binding depends upon whether or not they have attained the status of *de facto* districts. For a school district to be regarded as *de facto* three conditions must be met: (1) There must have existed some statute under which such a corporation could have been organized, (2) There must have been some attempt to organize the district under the statute, and (3) The district must have exercised the powers conferred upon it long enough to give rise to the reasonable assumption that it is the corporation it purports to be. When a district meets these three conditions it is a *de facto* district, at least, and, until it is put an end to by proper legal proceedings, its acts are as binding as they would have been if the district had been legally created in the first place.

Challenging the Legality of a District

The law provides a special action whereby the legality of a school district may be attacked. It is an action in the nature of *quo warranto* brought in the name of the state by the attorney-general or the state's attorney. The right to question the legality of a school district is the prerogative of the state and may not be exercised by a private party who has no interest in the matter distinct from that of the public in general. Nevertheless, it has been held that if two districts claim the same territory, one may bring a direct action against the other challenging its legality, and need not resort to an action in *quo warranto*.

II.

COURT DECISIONS

COURT DECISIONS

1. "The state, acting through the legislature, may create whatever type of local school administrative organization it may desire" (p. 3).

ATTORNEY GENERAL v. LOWREY,
199 U. S. 233 (1905)
(Decided by the Supreme Court of the United States)

[This was an action in *quo warranto* brought by the Attorney General of the State of Michigan questioning the right of certain school officers to hold office. Basic to this issue was the question of the legality of a school district known as "The Public Schools of the Village of Jerome."]

MR. JUSTICE MCKENNA delivered the opinion of the court.

. . . .

The grounds of attack upon the validity of the act creating the new district in the Supreme Court of the State were as follows:

First. It deprives this school district or municipality of the right of local self-government, guaranteed to all municipalities by the constitution.

Second. The title to the act indicates and the act itself embraces more than one object.

Third. The act is broader than the title; the body of the act embraces many objects not covered by the title.

Fourth. The act as passed impairs the obligation of contracts, within the meaning of the Constitution of the United States and the constitution of the State of Michigan.

With the first three grounds we have no concern. They present strictly local questions. We are concerned with the fourth ground only in so far as it invokes the Constitution of the United States. The Supreme Court disposed of this ground as follows: "We have already shown that the obligation of contracts is not impaired. The districts did not hold this property under any contract with the State, but as a public agency." In other words, the non-existence of a contract was rested on the construction of the constitution and laws of the State, and hence defendant in error contends that the decision of the court did not involve a Federal question. This, however, overlooks the power and duty of this court to determine for itself the existence or non-existence of a contract. Other grounds in support of the motion to dismiss are urged which, we think, are also untenable. The motion is therefore denied.

9

Plaintiff in error broadened in this court his objections to the act, based on the Constitution of the United States. He urges, besides, the contract clause of the Constitution, that provision of the Fourteenth Amendment which protects private property from deprivation without due process of law, and section 4, Article IV, which provides "The United States shall guarantee to every State in the Union a republican form of government." But the grounds all depend ultimately upon the same arguments. If the legislature of the State has the power to create and alter school districts and divide and apportion the property of such districts no contract can arise, no property of a district can be said to be taken, and the action of the legislature is compatible with a republican form of government even if it be admitted that section 4, Article IV, of the Constitution applies to the creation of, or the powers or rights of property of, the subordinate municipalities of a State. We may omit, therefore, that section and Article from further consideration. The decision of the other grounds urged we may rest upon the opinion of the Supreme Court of the State and the case of *Laramie County* v. *Albany County et al.*, 92 U. S. 307. It is there said in many ways, with citation of many supporting cases, that the legislature of a State has absolute power to make and change subordinate municipalities. The following quotation meets exactly the contentions of plaintiff in error:

"Institutions of the kind, whether called counties or towns, are the auxiliaries of the State in the important business of municipal rule, and cannot have the least pretension to sustain their privileges or their existence upon anything like a contract between them and the legislature of the State, because there is not and cannot be any reciprocity of stipulation, and their objects and duties are utterly incompatible with everything of the nature of compact. Instead of that, the constant practice is to divide large counties and towns, and to consolidate small ones, to meet the wishes of the residents, or to promote the public interests as understood by those who control the action of the legislature. Opposition is sometimes manifested but it is everywhere acknowledged that the legislature possesses the power to divide counties and towns at their pleasure and to apportion the common property and the common burdens in such manner as to them may seem reasonable and equitable." Many cases are cited. See also *Worcester* v. *Worcester Street Railway Co.*, 196 U. S. 539.

Judgment affirmed.

Guides for Class Discussion

1. What status did the court assign school districts?
2. What significance do you attach to the court's comments regarding contracts? Were they relevant?

3. To what conclusion do you come regarding the authority of the legislature to create school districts? Justify this conclusion.

2. ". . . *[the state] may designate as school districts such civil divisions . . . as towns, cities, townships, or counties*" (p. 3).

ASSOCIATED SCHOOLS OF INDEPENDENT DISTRICT NO. 63 v. SCHOOL DISTRICT NO. 83,
122 Minn. 254, 142 N.W. 325 (1913)
(Decided by the Supreme Court of Minnesota)

[In this case plaintiff, a consolidated school, maintained an agricultural and an industrial department. During the school year it furnished instruction in these departments to certain nonresident pupils. This action was brought to collect tuition, in the amount of $2.50 per month, per pupil, for eight pupils resident in defendant district. Defendant demurred on the ground that the complaint did not state a cause of action. In brief, the legality of the statute upon which plaintiff based its action was questioned. The lower court rendered a judgment for plaintiff, and the defendant appealed. The higher court affirmed the decision of the lower court. In so doing it commented on the authority of the legislature to establish school districts.]

HALLAM, J. . . .

. . . .

It is contended that to tax defendant district for tuition of pupils residing therein and attending plaintiff's school creates unequal taxation; that it constitutes the taking or appropriation of the money of the district without compensation and without due process of law, and without a hearing to defendant, and for a purpose it may not desire. These contentions cannot be sustained. They are based on too narrow a view of the power of the Legislature over its municipal sub-divisions and over matters of education.

It has never been doubted that the state has the power to require of its municipal subdivisions the performance of duties of state concern and to demand that they raise money by taxation and disburse the same for such purposes. These municipal subdivisions are mere auxiliaries of the state, created by the state as a means of exercising its political power in an orderly manner. Being thus subordinate agencies of the state, they are subject to the control and direction of the Legislature in matters of internal government, and the Legislature may require such public duties and functions to be performed by them as fall within the general scope and objects of municipal organizations.

The maintenance of public schools is a matter, not of local, but of state, concern. When the Constitution of Minnesota was adopted, its framers inserted these two provisions:

"The stability of a republican form of government depending mainly upon the intelligence of the people, it shall be the duty of the Legislature to establish a general and uniform system of public schools." Section 1, article 8.

"The Legislature shall make such provisions by taxation or otherwise, as, with the income arising from the school fund, will secure a thorough and efficient system of public schools in each township in the state." Section 3, article 8.

The object of these provisions is "to insure a regular method throughout the state, whereby all may be enabled to acquire an education which will fit them to discharge intelligently their duties as citizens of the republic." Board of Education of Saulk Centre v. Moore, 17 Minn. 412, 416 (Gil. 391, 394). These provisions were not a grant of power to the Legislature, for *all the powers there mentioned would have existed without such grant.* [Emphasis added.] They were inserted as a mandate to the Legislature, prescribing as a duty the exercise of this inherent power.

This statute is within the legislative power. This state has always imposed upon each community the burden of providing for the elementary education of its children. It has required school districts to maintain common schools for at least five months in the year . . . and to provide by taxation sufficient revenue therefor. . . . The power of the Legislature to make such requirement has never been doubted. It is equally within the power of the Legislature to provide that, if a district does not see fit to furnish school facilities of its own, it shall pay some other district for the furnishing of such facilities.

If this were a question of common school education, this proposition would probably not be questioned. But the power of the Legislature to impose a system of public school education upon local communities is not limited to common branches alone. It is the judgment of the Legislature that this state should now require public education in something more than the common branches; that it should provide for the public education of boys in that which pertains to successful agriculture, and of girls in that which pertains to successful housekeeping. The question whether the population and wealth of the state are such as to warrant such measures is a legislative and not a judicial question, a question of legislative policy and not of legislative power.

There is nothing in the statute in question that violates the constitutional requirement of equality of taxation. The law operates alike on all persons and property similarly situated. This is all that is required. . . . Nor does it violate the constitutional requirement of a "uniform system of public schools." In Curryer v. Merrill, 25 Minn. 1, 6, 33 Am. Rep. 450, the court said: "The rule of uniformity contemplated by this constitutional provision, which the Legislature is required to observe, has reference to the system which it may provide, and not to the district organizations that may be established under it. These may differ in respect to size, grade, corporate powers, and franchises, as may seem to the Legislature best, under different circumstances and conditions; but the principle of uniformity is not violated, if the system which is adopted is made to have a general and uniform application to the entire state, so that the same grade or class of public schools may be enjoyed by all localities similarly situated, and having the requisite conditions for that particular class or grade."

The view we have taken of this case is amply sustained by authority.

Guides for Class Discussion

1. What does this decision say about the legislature's authority to designate various governmental units as school districts?
2. What does it say with respect to the legislature's authority to create districts of different size?
3. What is the significance of the italicized statement in paragraph 6?
4. What is the authority for the court's reasoning as found in the italicized statement?

3. ". . . *districts may be created which have no territorial relation-ship to existing civil divisions of the state*" (p. 3).

DISTRICT TOWNSHIP OF UNION V. INDEPENDENT
DISTRICT OF GREENE,
41 Iowa 30 (1875)
(Decided by the Supreme Court of Iowa)

[This action involved the levying of a school tax. The question back of this, however, related to the legality of the creation of a school district. Relevant facts are brought out in the decision.]

DAY, J.—The claim of appellant is that the Board of Directors of the District township of Coldwater, Butler county, had no right, in laying off the boundaries of the Independent District of Greene, to incorporate into it territory in another county, without the consent or concurrence of the school district township, or other school authorities in the other county.

The school law evidently contemplates that school districts shall coincide in boundary with the civil townships. Sec. 1713 of the Code of 1873 provides: "Each civil township, now or hereafter organized . . . is hereby declared a school district for all the purposes of this chapter, subject to the provisions hereinafter made." The only exception which we are aware of to this requirement is created by section 1797 of the Code, as follows: "In cases where, by reason of streams or other natural obstacles, any portion of the inhabitants of any school district cannot, in the opinion of the county superintendent, with reasonable facility enjoy the advantages of any school in their township, the said county superintendent, with the consent of the Board of Directors of such district as may be affected thereby, may attach such part of said townships to an adjoining township, and the order therefor shall be transmitted to the secretary of each district, and be by him recorded in his records, and the proper entry made on his plat of the district." No such limitation, however, is placed upon the organization of inde-pendent districts. Section 1800 of the Code provides: "Any city or town containing not less than three hundred inhabitants within its limits, may be constituted a separate school district, and territory contiguous to such a city or town may be included with it as a part of said separate district in the manner hereinafter provided."

. . . .

If, then, an independent district can be formed out of parts of two townships, not before forming an independent organization, and with-out the concurrent act of the two townships, when they are situated in the same county, we are unable to see why the same thing may not be done when the two parts of townships are situated in different counties, for no greater restriction is imposed in the one case than in the other. Appellant refers to section 1812 of the Code, and insists that it contains the only conditions when and prescribes the only mode in which, an independent district can be formed of territory embraced in two counties. In this position we cannot concur. Section 1812 applies to the single case where under the laws of the state heretofore in force, school districts were formed of portions of two counties, and provides that steps may be taken for the organization of an independent district, upon the written request of five legal voters residing in portions of the territory in each county. The only thing that can be inferred from this section is that when these conditions exist the independent district must be formed in the manner in this section prescribed. It contains no express or implied provision that no independent district shall be formed of parts of two counties, except when these conditions exist.

Appellant says that a hundred illustrations might be made of the abuses and entanglements which would probably arise from the establishment of the rule contended for by the appellee. But the effect upon the inhabitants of the respective townships is the same, whether they are situated in the same or different counties. And it would not be difficult to furnish illustrations of the inconveniences and hardships which would attend the construction contended for by appellant, in cases where towns and cities are situated upon or near to the line between two counties.

We feel constrained to hold that the court rightly sustained the demurrer, and that the judgment should be

Affirmed.

Guides for Class Discussion

1. In light of this decision what authority does the state have with respect to the creation of school districts?

2. What did the courts say concerning "abuses and entanglements" which might arise from the establishment of school districts?

3. Considering this case was decided in 1875, do you think the courts would hold similarly today?

4. *"The local school corporation, whatever type it may be, is a quasi-corporation, or a quasi-municipal corporation, as distinguished from a municipal corporation proper"* (p. 3).

HELLER V. STREMMEL,

52 Mo. 309 (1873)
(Decided by the Supreme Court of Missouri)

[The question before the court was whether the Board of Presidents and Directors of the Public Schools was a municipal corporation, within the meaning of the law that provided that no person should be eligible for the office of justice of the county court who, at the time of his election, held any *municipal* office.]

VORIES, Judge, delivered the opinion of the court.

The plaintiff and the defendant were opposing candidates for the office of Justice of the County Court of St. Louis County, at an election holden on the first Tuesday after the first Monday of August, 1871. The certificate of election was given to the defendant, upon which he was commissioned and entered on the duties of the office.

The plaintiff filed his petition in the Circuit Court of St. Louis County, under the provisions of the statute, contesting the election of the plaintiff [*sic*] and averring as a ground of his contest of said election, that the defendant at the time of the election held the office, and still held the office, of a director in the "Board of the President and Directors of the St. Louis Public Schools," and that defendant was in virtue thereof ineligible to the office of Justice of the County Court, because it is provided by law, that "no person shall be eligible to the office of Justice of the County Court, who at the time of his election shall hold any office under any Municipal or Railroad Corporation created by the laws of the State of Missouri," and that "the Board of President and Directors of the St. Louis Public Schools" was a municipal corporation created by the laws of the State of Missouri.

The defendant demurred to the petition on the ground that it did not state any facts sufficient to entitle the plaintiff to contest the election, or to affect the defendant's right to the office. The St. Louis Circuit Court sustained the demurrer at Special Term, and rendered a final judgment against the plaintiff. The plaintiff appealed to the General Term of said Court, where said judgment was affirmed. The case has been brought to this Court by Writ of Error.

The only question presented to this Court by the plaintiff in error, is whether the defendant is disqualified or ineligible to hold the office of County Court Justice by virtue of his at the time of the election holding the office of School Director in "the Board of President and Directors of the St. Louis Public Schools." By an Act of the Legislature of the State of Missouri, entitled "an act concerning the County of St. Louis" approved March 14th, 1859, and the acts amendatory thereof, it is provided, that no person shall be eligible to the office of Justice of the County Court, "who at the time of his election shall hold any office under any Municipal or Railroad Corporation created by the laws of the State of Missouri." (Laws of Missouri 1859, page 449, also Session Acts 1863, page 158; Acts 1871, page 109.) It is contended by the plaintiff, that "the Board of President and Directors of the St. Louis Public Schools" is a municipal corporation, and that defendant being a Director in said Board, is not eligible to the office of Justice of the County Court.

A municipal corporation is defined by Bouvier to be: "A public corporation created by Government for political purposes, and having subordinate and local powers of legislation. An incorporation of persons, inhabitants of a particular place or connected with a particular district, enabling them to conduct its local, civil government." (2nd Bouvier's Law Dic., 21; see also 2 Kent, 317, p. 275.) "The Board of President and Directors of the St. Louis Public Schools" is not a corporation created for *political* purposes, nor is it created for the purpose of enabling the people of the District named, to conduct its local, *civil* government, and the mere fact that its limits of jurisdiction are the same as that of the City of St. Louis, makes no difference in that particular; it is just the same as if it had constituted a township, or any other district described, as a School District. The corporation is created to take charge and control of the public schools and make rules for the management of the schools, to take possession and charge of all lands and lots which have been received for the inhabitants of St. Louis for school purposes, and to dispose of the same, and apply the proceeds to purposes of education under the provisions of the act. In fact, the Corporation is created by the State to assist in carrying out the general common School system of education adopted by the State, and although the particular district is separately organized and incorporated by the Legislature, it is no more a *municipal corporation*, than is the Board of Directors of any other School District in the State.

The general accepted definition of a municipal corporation would only include organized cities and towns, and other like organizations, with political and legislative powers for the local, civil government and police regulations of the inhabitants of the particular district included in the boundaries of the corporation. It was such corporations, that I think, were intended by the Legislature in disqualifying persons to hold the office of Justice of the County Court, who at the time should hold an office in any municipal corporation. Justice Dillon, in his work on "Municipal Corporations," uses this language in defining a municipal corporation: "Thus an incorporated School District or county, as well as a city, is a public corporation; but the School District or County, properly speaking, is not, while the City is a municipal corporation."

Again in speaking of School Districts, Road Districts, Counties, Townships, etc. Judge Dillon says: "They are purely auxiliaries of the State, and to the General Statutes of the State they owe their creation, and the Statute confers all the powers they possess, prescribes all the duties they owe, and imposes all liabilities to which they are subject. Considered with reference to the limited number of their corporate powers, the bodies above named rank low down in the scale or corporate grade of corporate existence; and hence have been frequently termed *quasi* corporations. This designation distinguishes them, on the one hand from private corporations aggregate, and on the other from municipal corporations proper, such as cities or towns, acting under charters, etc." (Dillon on Municipal Corporations, pages 30 to 33.)

From the foregoing authorities as well as from the reason of the case, I am well satisfied that the term *municipal corporations* does not in its common acceptation or its legal sense include School Districts or corporations organized for the purposes of education only, either in connection with our Common School system or otherwise, and that the Legislature, in rendering officers of municipal corporations ineligible to the office of County Justice, never intended to include School Trustees.

The other Judges concurring, the judgment of the St. Louis Circuit Court is affirmed.

Guides for Class Discussion

1. If the school district is not a pure municipal corporation, how may it be characterized?
2. What is the significance of the quotation from Judge Dillon to the effect that school districts " 'rank low down in the scale or corporate grade of corporate existence' "?
3. How does one distinguish between municipal and quasi-municipal corporations?
4. Is this a real or a technical distinction? Give reasons.

5. "A *quasi-corporation is an agency of the state, created for the purpose of carrying into effect policies of state-wide concern*" (p. 3).

LINCKE V. MOLINE BOARD OF EDUCATION,
245 Ill. App. 459 (1927)
(Decided by the Appellate Court of Illinois)

[This action was brought by plaintiff to recover damages for injuries received when she fell on the steps of a high school building. The question involved was whether a school district could be held liable in such a case. Plaintiff contended that the district was governed by the rule regarding the liability of municipal corporations. Defendant contended that the district, as a quasi-municipal corporation, had the same immunity as the state. The court, therefore, found it necessary to consider the legal status of a school district.]

MR. JUSTICE JONES delivered the opinion of the court.

. . . .

The question involved in this case is whether a school board is liable in damages under such circumstances as are alleged in the declaration. It is urged that defendant in error is a municipal corporation and by statute is capable of suing and being sued; that it was acting in a proprietary capacity and is therefore liable.

There is definite distinction between the liability of voluntary municipal corporations, such as cities created for their own benefit, and involuntary *quasi* corporations established by law as civil divisions of the State. At common law, actions for a dereliction of duty were maintainable against the former, but the latter, existing only as an agency of the State, were not liable. Such is the rule in Illinois. . . . The ground of distinction is that public, involuntary, *quasi* corporations are mere political divisions of the State created by general laws to aid in the general administration of the government and are not so liable, while those that are liable have privileges conferred upon them at their request, constituting a consideration for the duties imposed upon them. . . .

In regard to public, involuntary, *quasi* corporations, the rule is that there is no implied liability imposed upon them. These, such as counties, townships, school districts, road districts and other similar *quasi* corporations exist under general laws of the State, with territory apportioned into local subdivisions for the purposes of civil and governmental administration. In such organizations the duties, and their correlative powers, are assumed *in invitum* and there is no responsibility to respond in damages in a civil action for neglect in the performance of duties, unless a right of action is given by statute. . . .

A board of education is a corporation or *quasi* corporation created *nolens volens,* by the general law of the State to aid in the administration of the State government, and charged, as such, with duties purely governmental in character. It owns no property, has no private corporate interests and derives no special benefits from its corporate acts. It is simply an agency of the State having existence for the sole purpose of performing certain duties, deemed necessary to the maintenance of an "efficient system of free schools" within the particular locality of its jurisdiction. The State acts in its sovereign capacity, and does not submit its action to the judgments of courts and is not liable for the torts or negligence of its agents, and a corporation created by the State as a mere agency for the more efficient exercise of governmental functions is likewise exempted from the obligation to respond in damages as master, for negligent acts of its servants to the same extent as is the State itself, unless such liability is expressly provided by the statute creating such agency.

Plaintiff in error urges that defendant in error was exercising an authorized proprietary function under section 115 of the School Law (Cahill's St. ch. 122, ¶ 123). It is elementary that the powers and duties of municipal corporations, such as cities, are of two kinds: 1st, public or governmental, and 2nd, private or proprietary. They are not liable for negligence when exercising governmental functions. When performing proprietary functions they are chargeable with the same duties and obligations as private corporations and ordinary individuals. School districts derive their existence and all their powers from the legislature and have no inherent powers. . . . They have only such powers as are conferred expressly or by necessary implication. . . . School districts are charged with duties purely governmental in character and are agencies of the State, existing for the sole purpose of performing duties in connection with the maintenance of an efficient system of free schools . . . and differ from cities and other municipal corporations which have power to function in certain private capacities.

It is urged by plaintiff in error that the provisions of section 115 of the School Law delegates a proprietary function to school directors and boards of education and that the declaration therefore states a cause of action within its terms. That section provides for granting the use of assembly halls and classrooms when not otherwise needed, including light, heat and attendants, for public lectures, concerts and other educational and social interests, under such provisions and control as they may see fit to impose, and to conduct or provide for the conducting of recreational, social and civic activities in the school buildings under their control; but it does not expressly nor by necessary implication authorize a grant for hire, reward, revenue or profit as charged in the declaration. Any different construction would be utterly at variance with the single purpose for which school districts are created and maintained, as expressed in the constitution and the statutes and as limited by repeated decisions of the courts of this State. The use of school property for such purposes is not out of harmony with the object for which schools are conducted, but stimulates and fosters the interest of the pupils and patrons and promotes the efficiency of public schools.

Guides for Class Discussion

1. What is a quasi-municipal corporation?
2. Distinguish between voluntary and involuntary corporations.
3. What relationship exists between a quasi-municipal corporation and the state?
4. What is the significance of the statement that the state "does not submit its action to the judgments of courts"?
5. Differentiate between "proprietary" and "governmental" functions.
6. What did the court mean when it said "school districts . . . have no inherent powers. . . ."?

6. ". . . *municipal corporations proper, such as towns and cities, are . . . created to enable local communities to regulate and administer their own peculiar local concerns*" (p. 3).

CITY OF WORCESTER v. WORCESTER CONSOLIDATED STREET RAILWAY CO.,
196 U.S. 539 (1905)
(Decided by the Supreme Court of the United States)

[The street railway failed to make repairs in the streets required of it by the city, when it permitted the company to extend its tracks, and the city brought action to compel the company to make the repairs in question. The company contended the city, as a municipal corporation, had no authority to enter into the contract relating to street railway locations. To settle the question, the court found it necessary to consider the nature of municipal corporations.]

Mr. Justice Peckham . . . delivered the opinion of the court.

. . . .

The contention on the part of the plaintiff in error is that, by virtue of the restrictions or conditions placed by it upon granting the various extensions of locations of the track of the railroad company, and by the acceptance of the same by the company, a contract was entered into between the city and the railroad company, which could not be altered without the consent of both parties, and that as the city had never consented to any alteration of the obligation of the railroad company to make repairs in the streets as provided for in those restrictions or conditions, the subsequent legislation contained in the act of 1898 impaired the obligation of that contract, and was therefore void, as a violation of the Constitution of the United States.

In the view we take of this subject it may be assumed, for the purpose of argument, that the city of Worcester had power, under the legislation of the State, to grant the right to extend the location of the railroad company's tracks upon the restrictions or conditions already mentioned. It may also be assumed, but only for the purpose of the argument, that the restrictions or conditions contained in the orders or decrees of the board of aldermen, upon their acceptance by the company, became contracts between the city and the company.

The question then arising is, whether the legislature, in the exercise of its general legislative power, could abrogate the provisions of the contract between the city and the railroad company with the assent of the latter, and provide another and a different method for the paving and repairing of the streets through which the tracks of the railroad company were laid under the permit of their extended location. We have no doubt that the legislature of the commonwealth had that power. A municipal corporation is simply a political subdivision of the State, and exists by virtue of the exercise of the power of the State through its legislative department. The legislature could at any time terminate the existence of the corporation itself, and provide other and different means for the government of the district comprised within the limits of the former city. The city is the creature of the State. . . . As is stated in *United States* v. *Railroad Company*, 17 Wall. 322, 329, a municipal corporation is not only a part of the State but is a portion of its governmental power. "It is one of its creatures, made for a specific purpose, to exercise within a limited sphere the powers of the State. The State may withdraw these local powers of government at pleasure, and may, through its legislature or other appointed channels, govern the local territory as it governs the State at large. It may enlarge or contract its powers or destroy its existence. As a portion of the State in the exercise of a limited portion of the powers of the State, its revenues, like those of the State, are not subject to taxation."

In *New Orleans v. Clark*, 95 U. S. 644, 654, it was stated by Mr. Justice Field, in delivering the opinion of the court, that:

"A city is only a political subdivision of the State, made for the convenient administration of the government. It is an instrumentality, with powers more or less enlarged, according to the requirements of the public, and which may be increased or repealed at the will of the legislature. In directing, therefore, a particular tax by such corporation, and the appropriation of the proceeds to some special municipal purpose, the legislature only exercises a power through its subordinate agent, which it could exercise directly; and it does this only in another way when it directs such corporation to assume and pay a particular claim not legally binding for want of some formality in its creation, but for which the corporation has received an equivalent."

In *Commissioners of Laramie County v. Commissioners of Albany County et al.*, 92 U.S. 307, it was held that public or municipal corporations were but parts of the machinery employed in carrying on the affairs of the State, and that the charters under which such corporations are created may be changed, modified or repealed as the exigencies of the public service or the public welfare may demand; that such corporations were composed of all the inhabitants of the territory included in the political organization; and the attribute of individuality is conferred on the entire mass of such residents, and it may be modified or taken away at the mere will of the legislature, according to its own views of public convenience, and without any necessity for the consent of those composing the body politic.

It was said in that case that "public duties are required of counties as well as of towns, as a part of the machinery of the State; and, in order that they may be able to perform those duties, they are vested with certain corporate powers; but, their functions are wholly of a public nature, and they are at all times as much subject to the will of the legislature as incorporated towns, as appears by the best text writers upon the subject and the great weight of judicial authority."

In *Commissioners etc. v. Lucas, Treasurer*, 93 U. S. 108, 114, the question of the validity of an act of the legislature was presented, and Mr. Justice Field, in delivering the opinion of the court, said:

"Were the transaction one between the State and a private individual, the invalidity of the act would not be a matter of serious doubt. Private property cannot be taken from individuals by the State, except for public purposes, and then only upon compensation or by way of taxation; and any enactments to that end would be regarded as an illegitimate and unwarranted exercise of legislative power. . . . But between the State and municipal corporations, such as cities, counties, and towns, the relation is different from that between the State and the individual. Municipal corporations are mere instrumentalities of the State, for the convenient administration of government; and their powers may be qualified, enlarged or withdrawn, at the pleasure of the legislature."

In *Mount Pleasant* v. *Beckwith*, 100 U.S. 514, it was held that, where no constitutional restriction is imposed, the corporate existence and powers of counties, cities and towns are subject to the legislative control of the State creating them.

In *New Orleans* v. *New Orleans Water Works Company*, 142 U.S. 79, it was also held that a municipal corporation was the mere agent of the State in its governmental character, and was in no contract relations with its sovereign, at whose pleasure its charter may be amended, changed or revoked without the impairment of any constitutional obligation. It was also therein held that such a corporation, in respect to its private or proprietary rights and interest, might be entitled to constitutional protection. The Massachusetts courts take the same view of such a corporation. *Browne* v. *Turner*, 176 Massachusetts, 9.

Enough cases have been cited to show the nature of a municipal corporation as stated by this court. . . .

Guides for Class Discussion

1. What is a municipal corporation?
2. What authority does the legislature have over municipal corporations?
3. Did the court distinguish between municipal and quasi-municipal corporations?
4. Compare this case with *Lincke* v. *Moline, supra.*

7. *"The state . . . may delegate its authority to establish districts to some administrative board or official"* (*pp. 3-4*).

ZAWERSCHNIK V. JOINT COUNTY SCHOOL COMMITTEE,
271 Wis. 416, 73 N.W. (2d) 566 (1955)
(Decided by the Supreme Court of Wisconsin)

[This action was an appeal from the orders of a joint school committee which had the effect of dissolving certain common school districts, detaching a part of a joint school district, and attaching and consolidating the districts so dissolved and detached to an existing district. Numerous grounds for the appeal were mentioned, only a few of which are considered here.]

STEINLE, Justice.

. . . .

In its determination of appellants' challenge to the order of the Joint Committee on ground of abuse of power upon bases as outlined above, the trial court properly applied principles of law that have become well-established in the jurisprudence of this state with reference to issues such as presented.

Of paramount importance here are the following considerations: The Legislature may vest power in proper boards or officers to establish school districts and change the boundaries of existing districts. . . . A county school committee (or joint committee) possesses the power to order the creation, alteration, consolidation or dissolution of school districts within its jurisdiction. Section 40.03 (1), Stats. Where different conclusions as to where the lines of a district should be, may be drawn from the evidence submitted, the conclusions adopted by the legislative body cannot be interfered with. . . . When it appears that a determination which is challenged as being unreasonable, arbitrary or an unequal exercise of power is actually fairly debatable, the court may not substitute its judgment for that of the legislative body charged with the primary duty and responsibility of determining the question. . . .

The duty of forming and altering school districts is purely municipal and administrative, and has no respect whatever to personal or property rights. . . .

The alteration of school districts in such manner and through such instrumentalities as the legislature prescribes is not the taking of property, nor does it deprive any person of his property, within the meaning of constitutional inhibitions in these respects, and statutes, in authorizing such changes in school districts, do not deny equal protection of law or due process of law? . . .

Whether the boundaries of a school district should be changed is not a question of law or fact for judicial determination, but purely a question of policy, to be determined by the legislative department. Such a matter presents a question of political expediency for the legislative department. The courts have nothing to do with the policy, wisdom, justice, fairness of such matters. They present questions for the consideration of those to whom the state has entrusted its legislative power, and their determination of them is not subject to review or criticism by the court. . . .

In State ex rel. Horton v. Brechler, 1925, 185 Wis. 599, 604, 605, 606, 202 N.W. 144, 146, it was said:

.   .   .   .

"The formation of school districts, however, is not a direct legislative function. Section 3, art. 10 state Constitution requires the Legislature to 'provide by law for the establishment of district schools, which shall be as nearly uniform as practicable.' From the very beginning of state government the power to form school districts has been conferred upon town boards—official bodies which are nearest to those who are interested in the formation of school districts. The Legislature has not attempted to set up any required standard or to make the action of the town board dependent upon the existence of any facts or circumstances. The town board has been permitted to exercise its discretion and form school districts that will in its best judgment promote the cause of education. From the earliest days the appeal from the decision of the town board in such matters to the state superintendent has been authorized. In State ex rel. Moreland v. Whitford, 54 Wis. 150, 11 N.W. 424, the power of the state superintendent in this respect was challenged as being unconstitutional. This court there held that his power was *quasi* judicial in nature and that it did not offend against any constitutional provisions."

.   .   .   .

A school district is a *quasi*-municipal corporation. It is an agent of the state for the purpose of administering the state's system of public education. . . .

In State ex rel. Zilisch v. Auer, supra [197 Wis. 284, 221 N.W. 864], the court quoted with approval the following statement in Hunter v. City of Pittsburgh, 207 U.S. 161, 178, 179, 28 S.Ct. 40, 52 L.Ed. 151:

" 'Municipal corporations are political subdivisions of the state, created as convenient agencies for exercising such of the governmental powers of the state as may be intrusted to them. . . . The state, therefore, at its pleasure, may . . . expand or contract the territorial area, unite the whole or a part of it with another municipality, repeal the charter and destroy the corporation. All this may be done, conditionally or unconditionally, with or without the consent of the citizens, or even against their protest. In all these respects the state is supreme, and its legislative body, conforming its action to the state Constitution, may do as it will, unrestrained by any provision of the Constitution of the United States. Although the inhabitants and property owners may, by such changes, suffer inconvenience, and their property may be lessened in value by the burden of increased taxation, or for any other reason, they have no right, by contract or otherwise, in the unaltered or continued existence of the corporation or its powers, and there is nothing in the Federal Constitution which protects them from these injurious consequences. The power is in the state, and those who legislate for the state are alone responsible for any unjust or oppressive exercise of it.' "

. . . .

In the light of these stated principles of law, the learned trial court in a comprehensive written opinion examined and analyzed in detail each objection raised by appellants in their challenge of the order of the Joint Committee, and upon such bases rendered its findings of fact, conclusions of law and order (judgment). The court determined that the Joint Committee had not abused or exceeded its power. Manifestly the matters considered and determined by the Joint Committee, were fairly debatable. We find no error with respect to the court's decision in this regard.

. . . .

The legislature within its discretion could have provided for the reorganization of school districts by school committees without referendum. The action of the school committee under such circumstances clearly would have been binding upon all taxpayers and electors of the several districts involved, without their having had a direct vote in the matter.

The consolidation of a smaller municipality with a larger one does not offend the constitution. . . .

. . . .

The residents and taxpayers have no vested inviolable rights in school district government. . . .

Guides for Class Discussion

1. What did the court say with respect to its authority to rule on matters related to the policy, justice, wisdom, and fairness of a particular school annexation or consolidation?
2. When may it interfere?
3. What did the court mean when it said: "The duty of forming . . . school districts . . . has no respect whatever to personal or property rights"?
4. Compare this decision with *Kenyon* v. *Moore, infra.*

8. "The state . . . may make the creation of a district contingent upon the consent of the inhabitants affected" (pp. 3-4).

STATE v. BOARD OF EDUCATION OF CITY OF CHETOPA,

173 Kan. 780, 252 P. (2d) 859 (1953)

(Decided by the Supreme Court of Kansas)

[This was an action to test the validity of a particular statute under which certain territory had been annexed to the school district of the City of Chetopa for school purposes. In ruling on the many questions involved, the court found it necessary to comment on the authority of the legislature to permit the inhabitants to approve plans for consolidation.]

WEDELL, Justice.

. . . .

Plaintiff asserts section 41 violates the due process clause of the federal constitution in that it fails to provide an impartial tribunal to determine whether the proposed attachment of the territory is ". . . proper and to the best interests of the schools of said city and territory. . . ." We shall not unduly labor this contention. The legislature has all the legislative power that exists. We know of nothing which prevents the legislature from designating the board of education as the proper agency for determining whether, in its judgment, the attachment of territory is to the best interests of the schools of the city and the attached territory. In the early case of State ex rel. Taylor v. Missouri P. Railway Co., 76 Kan. 467, 92 P. 606, involving the creation of a board of railroad commissioners, it was held:

"The act is not invalid because the constitution does not specifically provide for the creation of a board of railroad commissioners. The subjects upon which the legislature may enact laws are not enumerated in the constitution." (Syl. ¶ 4.)

But we need not pursue this subject. In section 41 the board is given no authority or power to make the exercise of its discretion final and conclusive. The legislature rested the final and ultimate decision with the electors in the school districts involved. The board is not obliged to approve the application of the electors to attach territory. Even, however, if the board approves the application only a petition signed by twenty-five per cent of the electors in the district is necessary to compel the submission of the entire matter to a vote in the district. Manifestly it cannot be said the electorate itself is a partial tribunal or that an opportunity of the electorate to make its own final decision in the premises constitutes an infringement of the due process clause of the federal constitution. Furthermore, should any board of education act fraudulently or in bad faith in the exercise of its discretion there is ample redress through the courts. . . .

· · · · · · · · · · · ·

The cases relied on by plaintiff are not controlling here and are of little help, if any, in view of entirely different provisions in the act now under scrutiny. Under section 41 of the instant act the board neither institutes nor passes on legislation of any kind or character. It originates nothing. It is not the moving party. It is merely an intermediary in one stage of the proceeding and without final authority, as will later appear, to effect the attachment of territory. It is the recipient of an application filed by a majority of the electors residing in the territory which such electors seek to have attached. The board is required to make a finding, favorable or unfavorable, on the application. In making such finding the board is merely executing the legislative will which, in effect, directs the board to exercise its discretion in determining whether in its judgment the attachment is proper and to the best interests of the schools of the city and the territory sought to be attached.

In a proper exercise of its discretion the board manifestly is obliged to consider numerous factors such as buildings and other physical equipment to accommodate additional students, the cost of new buildings or additions to old ones, if necessary, transportation problems, the sufficiency of its teaching force and many other practical matters involved in the proper maintenance, conduct and supervision of the school system. The exercise of that discretion does not differ substantially, if any, in character from the discretion it exercises in the performance of numerous other duties imposed upon it in the same act by the provisions of G.S. 1951 Supp. 72-1623 to 72-1626, inclusive. No rules or standards are prescribed for the board's determination of the numerous other duties prescribed in the statutes last mentioned. Shall we say the law prescribing these various statutory duties is void for the reason it is a delegation of legislative or administrative power without prescribed standards or rules to govern the board's judgment? We do not think so.

As heretofore stated, the legislature has not made it imperative that any application for attachment of territory be granted by the board. It often has been held that even the delegation of power to electors to petition designated tribunals to do certain things does not constitute a delegation of legislative power and that the action of the board or tribunal to which the petition is addressed is merely an administrative exercise of discretionary power. . . .

· · · · · · · · · · · ·

But we need not unduly prolong the discussion of delegation of legislative power. In view of other provisions of the instant law that subject really becomes an abstract question. As previously stated, a favorable decision by the board on the application in no sense is intended to be a finality under this law. In reality the board's action, if favorable, amounts to no more than an expression of its opinion or judgment and a willingness to have the territory in question attached.

Under our early school laws the school board took the initiative in certain attachment proceedings. In 1925 some of our laws were changed so as to enable a majority of the electors to apply for attachment of adjacent territory and the territory was attached if in the judgment of the board of education of a city it would be to the best interests of the city schools and the attached territory. The approval by the board ended the proceedings. . . .

However, under the instant law the judgment of the board need not be a finality. As already indicated only twenty-five per cent of the electors of a district are required to object to the board's judgment in order to compel the entire matter to be submitted to an election in the territory seeking attachment. If only a majority of those voting in such election are opposed to the attachment the order of the board is ineffective. It thus becomes clear that under this law we have a new feature which gives the electors within the district, rather than the board, the right to make the final decision. In State ex rel. v. Lamont, 105 Kan. 134, 181 P. 617, involving the right of electors to determine whether they would organize a school district, it was said:

"So it may be said here that the will of the petitioners does not govern, but when the provision made by the Legislature is accepted by the electors themselves by the proper vote, it becomes operative. The Legislature gives them permission to form themselves into such district, and when, by the proper election, they avail themselves of this permission, they are not exercising legislative power, but merely accepting a privilege conferred by a proper exercise of such power. Such granted permission is one means by which the Legislature has seen fit to obey the constitutional mandate to promote education, and such provision is not a violation of the Constitution." 105 Kan. at page 138, 181 P. at page 618.

. . . .

We believe it untenable to hold a law which permits the question of attachment of territory to be decided finally by the popular vote of the electors within the territory seeking attachment is a delegation of legislative power. [Emphasis added.] We are satisfied section 41 of the instant act does not violate article 2, section 1, of our constitution. Moreover, if courts entertain any doubt on that subject it is always resolved in favor of validity. Statutes are not stricken down unless the infringement of the superior law is clear beyond reasonable doubt. . . .

Guides for Class Discussion

1. Compare this case with *Zawerschnik* v. *Joint County School Committee, supra.*
2. What did the court say about the right of the legislature to delegate its authority to establish districts to some administrative body?
3. What did the court have to say about the fact the legislature omitted any rules or standards to guide the board as it exercised its discretion in forming school districts?
4. Compare this case with *Kenyon* v. *Moore, infra.*

9. *"When the state makes use of some administrative board or official in the establishment of school districts, care must be taken not to confer upon such board or official legislative authority . . . [because] the legislature . . . may not delegate legislative authority"* (*p. 4*).

KENYON V. MOORE,
287 Ill. 233, 122 N.E. 548 (1919)
(Decided by the Supreme Court of Illinois)

[This was an action attacking the record of the organization of a community high school district. Specifically it was contended that the law under which the district was organized was unconstitutional because it delegated legislative power to the county superintendent of schools. It gave power to him, upon receipt of a petition to create a district, to consider the form, size, and number of pupils and decide whether the district petitioned for was adequate. The lower court held the law unconstitutional and the higher court agreed.]

DUNCAN, C. J. . . .

. . . .

. . . Section 89 as amended violates article 3 of the Constitution because it delegates legislative powers to the county superintendent of schools. That section is silent as to the area, assessed valuation, and number of prospective high school pupils, as well as the form and size of the proposed district requisite to the formation of a satisfactory and efficient high school district. Those questions are delegated to the several county superintendents, with direction to them, before calling an election, to consider the form, size, and assessed valuation of the proposed district and the number of prospective high school pupils, "and if in his judgment the proposed district does not meet the requirements heretofore specified," he may refer the petition back to the petitioners with recommendations or may deny the prayer of it altogether. The requisites of a district are not theretofore specified that will make a satisfactory and efficient high school. This statute was not complete when it left the Legislature. It attempted to confer on county superintendents, a discretion as to what the law should be. That cannot be done. . . . The law as to what will constitute a satisfactory and efficient high school district is not found in the statute itself. It does not define or specify the requisite of a satisfactory and efficient community high school district, but leaves that matter to the discretion of the county superintendent without any rules of limitation for the exercise of such discretion. Until that official acts it cannot be known what the law is. Instead of being a uniform law, applicable alike to all similar areas of territory throughout the state, it is subject to the varying opinions of the county superintendents in the several counties of the state and of the same county superintendent or his successor in different parts of the same county. It is an arbitrary discretion and renders the section invalid because it delegates legislative powers to the county superintendent and of the opportunity it affords for unjust discrimination. . . .

Appellant cites People v. Buskirk, 279 Ill. 203, 116 N.E. 683, in support of his contention that he is only authorized by section 89 to decide questions as a ministerial, and not as a legislative, officer. In that case the questions of facts to be determined by the county superintendent were specified in the statute which provided for the organization of the district. The statute provided also for an appeal to the county superintendent of schools. It was his duty, under the law, to determine whether the petition was signed by more than two-thirds of the legal voters residing within the territory of the proposed new district. We there held that the county superintendent was not exercising judicial power, but that his action was administrative, every act which he was called upon to perform being directed by the statute, which prescribed the requisites required for the organization of a valid school district. That case is in no way controlling in this case, as all the facts requisite to the formation of a district, which are to be determined by the county superintendent, are not specified in section 89 of the statute now under consideration.

There are further objections made to the validity of section 89, one being that no valid election could be held under said section, as no provision is made for the appointment of judges and clerks to conduct the election. As the section is clearly unconstitutional, the record of the district in question was properly quashed by the circuit court upon that ground, and it will not be necessary to consider the further grounds argued by the attorneys in this case for and against the validity of the act.

The judgment of the circuit court in quashing the record is affirmed.

Judgment affirmed.

Guides for Class Discussion

1. Under what, if any, conditions may the legislature delegate legislative powers?
2. What is the reason back of this rule?
3. What kind of powers may the legislature delegate?
4. Differentiate between legislative and ministered powers.
5. Compare this case with *Zawerschnik* v. *Joint County School Committee, supra.* Can the two be reconciled?
6. Compare it with *State* v. *Board of Education of City of Chetopa, supra.*

10. "Where . . . the legislature restricts the discretion of the administrative agency [to whom it delegates authority to create a school district] by requiring it to act within the limits of designated policies or standards, the authority exercised is administrative and [the agency's actions] will be sustained by the courts, as long as it conforms to the statute" (p. 4).

Board of Education of Wellington Community Unit School District v. County Board of School Trustees,

13 Ill. App. (2d) 561, 142 N.E. (2d) 742 (1957)
(Decided by the Appellate Court of Illinois)

[This was an action to appeal an order of the County Board of School Trustees of Vermilion County (Illinois) directing that certain territory be detached from the Wellington School District and annexed to the East Lynn School District. Plaintiffs contended that the county board had failed to follow the policies or standards set up by the legislature. The lower court affirmed the order of the county board, but the higher court, here, reversed the decision of the lower court.]

ROETH, Justice.

. . . .

Essentially, the appellants here, being the Wellington Community Unit School District No. 7, and other objectors to the detachment and annexation, assert three grounds for reversal of the order of the Circuit Court. First, it is contended that the order entered by the County Board of School Trustees is erroneous and invalid for the reason that at the hearing the board refused to have the witnesses placed under oath prior to hearing their testimony, and secondly and related to the first point, it is the contention that the proceedings before the board could not result in a valid order for the reason that the board refused the appellants the right to cross-examination of the witnesses. Appellants, through their counsel, made timely objection to procedure adopted by the County Board of School Trustees and we think the questions presented were properly preserved for review. Finally, the order of the County Board of School Trustees contains no findings of fact or conclusions of law as a basis for the order and this is asserted as the third ground for error on this appeal.

. . . .

The procedure outlined in the statute was followed in this case insofar as the mechanical aspects thereof are concerned. Two vital elements, however, were missing from the "hearing" before the County Board of Trustees. The record on this case indicates that the County Board did not swear, or have sworn, any witnesses who appeared in support of or in opposition to the petition, and further that they refused the right of cross-examination of witnesses with a single exception.

We view the question presented on this appeal to be narrowed down to one of determining whether or not, in arriving at a decision on a petition filed in accordance with Article 4B of the School Code, as it existed at the time this petition was filed, the County Board of School Trustees may act upon the petition following a course of procedure as hereinabove outlined.

It is fundamental that the state may, with or without the consent of the inhabitants of a school district, and with or without notice or hearing, take the school facilities in the district without compensation and vest them in other districts or agencies. This is for the reason that a school district as such owns no property. All school facilities, such as grounds, buildings, equipment and so forth are in law and in fact the property of the state of Illinois, and subject to the legislative will. . . .

In passing upon petitions for annexation or detachment of a territory, the County Board of School Trustees can either allow or deny the petition before it, but cannot modify. The function of passing upon a petition is neither a delegation of legislative nor judical power. . . . Since the legislature may, in its wisdom, change, alter or modify the boundaries of school districts, it is obvious that it can authorize the discharge of this administrative duty, by other agencies and prescribe for them general standards to be followed in the execution of the delegated function. It has previously been determined that the standards prescribed in Article 4B are sufficient to serve as an adequate guide for the administrative body. . . .

The County Board of School Trustees is an administrative agency. . . . As such it is an arm of the legislative branch of government. However, in authorizing the administrative agency to act, the legislature has set up certain standards, attached certain conditions and required determination of certain facts. To this end it has provided for a hearing and notice thereof, required the hearing of evidence, and provided for a review of the action taken. The *proceedings* therefore, before the County Board of School Trustees are quasi judicial in character. . . .

In prescribing such a procedure, we can only presume that the legislature intended to place the whole administrative machinery into the well-defined, orderly proceeding commonly applicable to such proceedings.

* * * * * * * * * * * * * * * * * * *

In Chicago & E. I. Ry. Co. v. Commerce Commission, 341 Ill. 277, 173 N.E. 380, it was held that the making of findings (the determination of certain facts) by an administrative agency, necessitates the hearing of evidence with an opportunity to all parties to know of the evidence to be submitted or considered, to cross-examine witnesses, to inspect documents and to offer evidence in explanation or rebuttal.

It is axiomatic that the words of a statute will be construed in their ordinary sense and with the meaning commonly attributed to them unless such construction will defeat the manifest intention of the legislature.

* * * * * * * * * * * * * * * * * * *

In Jones v. Gregory, 48 Ill. App. 228, the court held the term evidence included the statements of a witness *under oath,* documentary evidence and whatever might be otherwise inspected by the trier of facts. . . .

A careful review of the record in this case does not indicate that there was a "hearing" within the above definitions. On the contrary, there was only a meeting of the Board of School Trustees wherein a parade of proponents and opponents—to the petition stated their wishes. These persons were not under oath. They were not subject to cross-examination that can be so helpful in ascertaining fact, not mere opinion. The hearing here is a statutory hearing wherein the term "hearing" must mean orderly proceeding. The term "evidence" must refer to the commonly accepted definition of that word. The procedure here is not in keeping with either.

Guides for Class Discussion

1. What does this case have to say with respect to the method of creating school districts?
2. To what extent must an administrative agency charged with creating school districts follow the statute?
3. In authorizing the administrative agency to create school districts what kind of power did the legislature delegate to it?
4. What kind of power must the legislature not delegate to such agencies?

11. "*. . . with the creation of . . . [school] districts, the courts have no concern; and they will not review an administrative agency's action in creating a district, in the absence of statute giving them that authority, unless it can be shown that the agency acted in a fraudulent, arbitrary, or unreasonable manner*" (p. 4).

THORLAND v. INDEPENDENT CONSOLIDATED SCHOOL DISTRICT,
246 Minn. 96, 74 N.W. (2d) 410 (1956)
(Decided by the Supreme Court of Minnesota)

[This was an action to test the legality of an order creating a consolidated school district. The lower court set aside the order, and the consolidated district appealed. The Supreme Court affirmed the decision of the lower court. Basic to this case was the issue of the authority of the court to review the actions of an administrative body charged with the responsibility of creating school districts.]

KNUTSON, Justice.

These are appeals from orders and judgment of the district court setting aside a proceeding for the consolidation of a number of school districts in Freeborn County.

.   .   .   .

. . . appellant contends that § 122.32 (3) has no application to consolidation proceedings and that the court has no right to review the proceeding on its merits. We do not believe that appellant's contentions are tenable. The right of review in such school district proceedings is purely a matter of statute.

Here the legislature has provided the grounds of appeal in § 122.32 and has adopted those grounds by reference in § 122.21. It is not for the courts to eliminate one of the grounds so provided unless the legislature, by so doing, has gone beyond the powers vested in it by the constitution. We therefore hold that the court on appeal has the same jurisdiction in reviewing an order of consolidation as it has in reviewing an order of the board of county commissioners in the formation of school districts as provided in § 122.32.

The next contention of appellant involved a determination of several questions incidental to the main one, which have been troublesome from the very early times. How far a court may go in setting aside an order of consolidation or an order of the county board, what quantum of proof is required, and what are the respective functions and scope of review of the trial court and this court are not so clearly defined by statute or by our decisions.

In the determination of these questions, certain fundamental rules of law must always be kept in mind. A school district, if technically not a municipal corporation, at least is a public corporation. School districts are subject to the control of the legislature, and their boundaries or territorial jurisdictions may be enlarged, diminished, or abolished in such manner and through such instrumentalities as the legislature may prescribe, except as limited by the constitution.

Determination of the question of formation or alteration of school districts by the agency to which action is entrusted by the legislature involves a legislative action.

Inasmuch as the action of such agency is legislative, the contention that to permit the court to determine whether such action is for the best interests of the territory affected permits the courts to invade the legislative field and thereby run afoul of the constitution is, as we said in Schweigert v. Abbott, 122 Minn. 383, 387, 142 N.W. 723, 724, not without merit. We there considered this question and disposed of it as follows:

". . . Whether public interests require and justify the organization of municipal or quasi municipal corporations, including school districts, is a matter purely for the Legislature, and cannot be conferred upon the courts. State v. Simons, 32 Minn. 540, 21 N.W. 750. If such authority cannot be directly conferred upon the courts . . . it would seem that an indirect method of conferring such jurisdiction would be equally invalid. . . . The court will, however, in determining whether the best interests of the territory affected justify a particular consolidation, limit its inquiry to the question whether the proceedings were arbitrary, resulting in unnecessary injustice to those who complain. In short, the court will be guided by the rule under which the organization of municipal corporations by county commissioners is set aside by the courts as arbitrary and unreasonable. . . ." This rule, we think, is in harmony with the great weight of authority.

The discretion vested in the county board or other agency to which such legislative action is given must be fairly exercised in good faith for the best interests of the people in the districts affected. As long as it is so exercised, the courts will not interfere but, when it is exercised in a fraudulent, arbitrary, or unreasonable manner so as to constitute an abuse of discretion, then it generally is held that the courts may and will interfere on behalf of the district or the voters injured thereby.

The scope of review of the district court on appeal has been stated so frequently that it would seem unnecessary to repeat it again, but the frequency with which this question arises and is presented here indicates that it is not understood fully as yet by litigants and courts alike. Probably a restatement of the fundamental law will serve to clarify the matter to some extent. . . .

. . . .

In Severts v. County of Yellow Medicine, 148 Minn. 321, 324, 181 N.W. 919, 921, we said:

". . . the County Board, in determining the propriety of enlarging a School District, exercises a discretion that is legislative, not judicial, and that on appeal to the district court, the determination of the Board is not reviewed as a judicial decision but as legislative action and that the inquiry on appeal is whether the determination of the County Board was based upon an erroneous theory of law or was arbitrary or fraudulent or oppressive, or in unreasonable disregard of the best interests of the territory affected."

On appeal to the district court there is no trial de novo, but the review is limited to a determination of whether the legislative agency has abused its discretion or has acted on an erroneous theory of law.

While the legislature cannot confer upon the courts legislative power, it can and does give to the court power to review the action of the administrative agency upon which it has conferred the legislative power to the extent that the courts will decide whether there has been an abuse of discretion vested in such agency. The power of review does not encompass the legislative function of determination but, rather, the power to prevent the administrative agency from exceeding its power by an arbitrary abuse of discretion. Thus, instead of an original right to determine, the court's function is to provide a check upon the arbitrary abuse of power vested in the agency entrusted by the legislature with the power of determination. In other words, the court's function, rather than being one of original determination, is to prevent the improper determination by the administrative agency.

Guides for Class Discussion

1. According to this decision what authority does the court have to create school districts?
2. Can the legislature delegate authority to create school districts? Why or why not?
3. If the legislature delegates the authority to create school districts to an administrative agency, what authority do the courts have over such agencies?
4. Do you think this decision is "good law"? Give reasons.
5. What is meant by "trial de novo"?

12. *"The provisions of a statute providing for the establishment of school districts with the consent of the residents of the territory affected must be strictly followed" (p. 4).*

BOARD OF EDUCATION OF COMMUNITY CONSOLIDATED SCHOOL DISTRICT 606 v. BOARD OF EDUCATION OF COMMUNITY UNIT SCHOOL DISTRICT 124,

11 Ill. App. (2d) 408, 137 N.E. (2d) 721 (1956)
(Decided by the Appellate Court of Illinois)

[This action was brought to have an election regarding school annexation declared void. The lower court held for plaintiffs, but the decree was reversed by the higher court. In doing so, the court reasoned that the resident voters acted as the agents of the legislature, and, in the absence of a showing that the statutory procedure was not followed, the acts of the voters determined all questions relative to annexation.]

CARROLL, Justice.

. . . .

. . . Section 1 of Article VIII of the Constitution of 1870 provides: "The general assembly shall provide a thorough and efficient system of free schools, whereby all children of the state may receive a good common school education."

The effect of this constitutional mandate is to require the legislature in the exercise of its powers to establish by appropriate legislative enactment a system of free schools. To meet the responsibility thus enjoined upon it, the legislature has provided for the creation of school districts. A district thus created is a quasi-municipal corporation or minor subdivision of the state and serves as an administrative arm of the legislature in putting into effect the will and intention of that body. . . .

The area comprising a school district may be divided, contracted or abolished at the will of the legislature. . . . In exercising control over the territory comprising a particular district, the resident voters thereof become the agents of the legislature. *By following the procedure prescribed by enabling legislation the voters of such district meet the responsibility of determining all questions relative to its boundaries.* [Emphasis added.] The theory behind this legislative policy is that the settlement of all questions relative to boundaries of a school district should be left to the resident voters thereof. . . .

When in pursuance of a valid legislative enactment these voters act upon a proposition to alter the boundaries of a school district, they do so as the agents of the legislature. As was said in People v. Deatherage, supra, "Those voters, in a practical sense, become administrative functionaries to administer the law."

The section of the school code pursuant to which the election in controversy was conducted has been held valid. . . . The election was not contested and failure to comply with the provisions of the statute is not charged in this action. Since the detachment proceedings were conducted in full compliance with the statute authorizing the same, it follows that the voters of the detached areas in exercising the authority thereby vested in them, were acting as the agents of the legislature in administering a provision of the school law. In so doing they were discharging a governmental function.

. . . .

Here we are not concerned. . . with the question as to whether the action of a school officer in making a change in district boundaries amounted to an abuse of the discretion vested in him. The action of which plaintiffs complain was that of the voters in effecting a detachment of territory from one district and annexing the same to another adjacent district under a valid statute enabling them to do so.

The alleged disastrous result upon the remaining territory of District 606 accomplished by the election and of which plaintiffs complain are of no consequence in determining the question of the authority of a chancery court to grant the relief prayed.

. . . Sec. 4B-6 provides that only the voters of the territory sought to be detached and of the district to which the territory is to be annexed shall vote upon the detachment proposition. If it was the intention of the legislature to give recognition to the wishes of the inhabitants of all of the district from which territory is detached, then provision therefor would be found in the Act. Injection of such requirement by the courts would constitute an unwarranted interference with legislative power.

Guides for Class Discussion

1. Compare this case with *Board of Education of Wellington Community School District* v. *County Board of School Trustees, supra.*
2. What single general principle can be drawn from this case and the *Board of Education of Wellington Community School District* case, *supra?*
3. What does this decision reveal concerning the authority of the courts over the subject of the creation of school districts?
4. As a result of this decision may it be said that the voters have an inherent right to approve the organization or creation of a school district?

13. *"If a petition is required for the calling of an election to determine the will of the inhabitants, the filing of the petition is jurisdictional, and any election held without the required petition having been filed is void"* (p. 4).

MESQUITE INDEPENDENT SCHOOL DISTRICT V. GROSS,
123 Tex. 49, 67 S.W. (2d) 242 (1934)
(Decided by Commission of Appeals of Texas, Section A)

[The school district brought this action against Gross to recover school taxes in the amount of $57.12 for the year 1928. Defendant specifically denied that the lands on which the taxes had been levied and which he owned were within the boundary of the plaintiff district. The plaintiff district contended that it had annexed the lands in question. Defendant, however, contended that the annexation was illegal. His defense to the action here, then, was that the plaintiff district was illegally constituted. At the root of the matter was the question of the legality of plaintiff as a school district. The lower court ruled in favor of Gross, and the district appealed to the Court of Civil Appeals. This court in turn certified the case to the Supreme Court on the ground it thought it advisable, because of the importance of the questions involved and because of doubtful meanings of certain language in the statute, that certain questions be decided by the Supreme Court.]

CRITZ, Judge.

This case is before the Supreme Court on certified questions from the Court of Civil Appeals for the Fifth district at Dallas. . . .

. . . .

The rule is well settled in this state that, when the creation of a public corporation, municipal, or quasi municipal, is authorized by statute, and such a corporation has been organized under color of such authority, its corporate existence cannot be attacked in a collateral proceeding. . . . In the case at bar Gross is resisting the claim of the Mesquite independent school district for taxes on the ground that the order purporting to add the territory in question to such district was and is void. Such a defense is a collateral attack on the order involved, and, if the board of trustees of the Mesquite independent school district acted under color of law in making it, such defense cannot be allowed.

It is also well settled that a school board is a creature of statute, and only has such jurisdiction as is expressly given it by statute, or is implied as a necessary incident to the jurisdiction so expressly given. . . . Such boards have no inherent power to detach territory from an adjoining district and add it to their own. In this connection we hold that such power is conferred by statute, and, being a special grant of authority, must be exercised in strict conformity with the mandatory direction of the statute. . . . When such a board acts without authority of law, express or implied, it acts without potential jurisdiction, and want of potential jurisdiction renders an act utterly void, and subject to collateral attack. . . .

When we come to examine the statute . . . we find that it does not purport to confer or grant unlimited power or jurisdiction on the school boards there mentioned to detach territory from other districts and add same to their own. On the other hand, such power of jurisdiction is expressly limited. One of the limitations expressly provided by the statute is that "a majority of such qualified voters sign a petition to that effect, any three of such qualified voters may file with the president of the board of trustees of such incorporated town or village the said petition, fully describing by metes and bounds the territory proposed to be annexed and showing its location with reference to the existing territory of the town or village already incorporated, provided that said territory proposed to be added must be contiguous to one line of said corporation." The plain words of the statute limit the potential jurisdiction of the school boards to instances where it is presented with the statutory petition. If the statutory petition is absent, the jurisdiction of the board is utterly lacking. In other words, unless and until the board is presented with the statutory petition, it has no jurisdiction in the premises.

When we come to examine the petition for annexation in the present case, we find that it fails to meet the statutory requirement that it fully describe by metes and bounds the territory sought to be annexed. A reading of the certificate thoroughly demonstrates this. Such being the case, the board was without potential jurisdiction to make the order of annexation. This being the case, the board acted without color of authority. Since the board acted without color of authority, and without potential jurisdiction, its order was and is utterly void, and subject to collateral attack. Since the order was and is utterly void and subject to collateral attack, it could not possibly be made valid by any act of the taxpayer. This holding settles the case adversely to the school board, and renders the other questions certified immaterial.

Guides for Class Discussion

1. Compare this case with *Spilker* v. *Bethel Special School District, infra.*
2. Compare it with *Walker Reorganized School District* v. *Flint, infra.*
3. What did the court rule with respect to the right to question the legality of a school district collaterally?
4. What did the court have to say with respect to the question of who had inherent authority to change the boundaries of school districts?
5. What did it say with respect to statutory restrictions placed upon a local school board's jurisdiction in the matter of changing boundaries?

14. "*Anyone who signs a petition may withdraw his name . . . at any time before action has been taken by those to whom the petition is addressed . . .*" (p. 4).

SCHOOL DISTRICT V. RENICK,
83 Okla. 158, 201 P. 241 (1921)
(Decided by the Supreme Court of Oklahoma)

[This action began when School District No. 24 of Custer County brought an action against the county superintendent to enjoin her from calling a meeting of the voters of certain districts to discuss the formation of a consolidated school district including, among others, District 24. This proposed meeting was in response to petitions which had been circulated throughout various school districts asking the superintendent to call the voters together to vote upon the question of consolidation. More than one-half of all the voters had signed the petitions. They were filed with the county superintendent between October 16 and 19, 1920. On October 20, 1920, before the petitions had been acted upon by the county superintendent, 30 of the 35 voters who were resident in District 24 asked to have their names withdrawn from the petition. She ignored the application of the 30 signers and proceeded to call the election. It was to prevent the holding of the election that this action was brought.]

MILLER, J. . . .

. . . .

The only question presented here that is necessary for us to pass upon is whether or not these persons who had signed the petition could withdraw their names from the petition before the county superintendent had acted upon it by calling the election.

The evidence of the county superintendent discloses that she had not yet called the election. . . .

. . . .

In state ex rel. Andrews v. Boyden et al., 21 S. D. 6, 108 N.W. 897, 15 Ann. Cas. 1122, the syllabus reads:

"Under the provision of the South Dakota Constitution that whenever a majority of the legal voters of a county shall petition the board of county commissioners to change the location of the county seat the board shall submit the question to the voters at the next general election, the signers of such a petition have the right to withdraw their names before final action has been taken thereon, and withdrawn names cannot be counted to make up the requisite number of voters."

In Malcomson v. Strong et al., 245 Ill. 166, 91 N. E. 1036, paragraphs 1 and 2 of the syllabus read:

"Voluntary subscribers to a petition may withdraw their names at any time before it is finally acted on.

"Where highway commissioners merely meet and note that a petition has been filed, fix a date for its consideration, and order the town clerk to give notice, it is not such final action thereon as deprive subscribers of the right to withdraw."

. . . .

In People ex rel. Koensgen et al. v. Strawn et al., 265 Ill. 292, 106 N. E. 840, paragraph 12 of the syllabus reads:

"A petition for the organization of a school district, which after certain names had been withdrawn therefrom was without a majority of the legal voters, left the trustees without jurisdiction to proceed, so that an order creating the district was void."

We do not think it is necessary for a person to give any reason why he withdraws his name from a petition thus signed by him where no action has been taken on the petition. It is not for a court to determine whether his reason for withdrawing his name is sufficient or not. He was induced to sign the petition under some representations made by the person or persons seeking his signature. The ingenious argument that may have been made to induce him to sign the petition was probably sufficient to satisfy his mind and he acted upon the representations made in such argument. He may find out that he has acted on a misapprehension of the facts or that the results to be obtained are not as he understood them in his own mind. Where the petition has not been acted upon by the officers clothed with the authority to act upon it, a signer has an absolute right to withdraw his name from the petition. It is not within the province of any court to inquire into the psychology of his mind or the sufficiency of his reasons for withdrawing his name from the petition.

It is conceded that if these names are legally withdrawn there is not a sufficient number of petitioners to authorize the election to be called so as to include school district No. 24 in the proposed consolidated district. These signers had withdrawn their names from the petition; therefore their names could not be counted, and the county superintendent was without authority to call any election for the consolidating of school districts which would include school district No. 24.

Guides for Class Discussion

1. Do you agree with this decision? Give reasons.
2. What is the effect of the discussion by the court concerning

the necessity of one's giving a reason for withdrawing his name from a petition?

3. Would the court have held differently had the county superintendent taken action on the petition previous to the time the request was made for the withdrawal of the signatures?

15. *"Statutory provisions with respect to the giving of notice of an election are mandatory and must be substantially followed or the election will be void"* (*pp. 4-5*).

STATE v. CONSOLIDATED INDEPENDENT SCHOOL DISTRICT,
246 Iowa 566, 68 N.W. (2d) 305 (1955)
(Decided by the Supreme Court of Iowa)

[This was an action challenging the legality of a newly formed consolidated school district. One of the main reasons for the challenge was that it was contended that the county superintendent, in having certain notices, including the notice of the election to approve consolidation, published in the *Waverly Democrat* of Waverly, Iowa, acted illegally. The statute provided that such notices must be published " 'in a newspaper published within the territory described in the petition, or *if none be published therein, in the next nearest town or city* in any county in which any part of the territory . . . is situated. . . .' (Emphasis supplied.)" No newspaper was published in the territory and it was conceded that the *Tripoli Leader,* published in Tripoli, Iowa, met the statutory requirements. The question before the court was whether the superintendent's action in having the notices published in the *Waverly Democrat,* rather than the *Tripoli Leader,* acted to invalidate the election.]

SMITH, Justice.

.   .   .   .

Code section 276.11, I.C.A., provided the county superintendent shall call an election "when the boundaries . . . have been determined," . . . "by giving notice . . . in the same newspaper as previous notices concerning it have been published. . . ."

This notice was published in the Waverly Democrat, and the election was held September 30, 1952. There is no controversy over the details or result of the election. The proposition to establish the consolidated independent district carried by a majority of five of the votes from outside the town of Readlyn, and 133 of those within the town limits.

When such a consolidation proposition carries Code section 276.18, I.C.A., required a special election to be called for election of directors "by giving notice by one publication in the same newspaper in which the former notices were published." Such election was held October 18, 1952, in the instant case upon publication of the notice in the Waverly Democrat.

The present proceeding was initiated December, 1952, and trial was commenced December 22, 1953. Decree was filed January 21, 1954, holding that the "purported Consolidated Independent School District of Readlyn, Bremer County, Iowa, is a de facto public corporation, and as such is performing the services and duties, and exercising the privileges of a school corporation."

The decree holds further that because of the failure "to observe the mandatory statutory provisions as to publications of notices . . . there was a failure to substantially comply with the law in such respect, and that such failure prevented a de jure formation of the said purported district. . . ."

.   .   .   .

The trial court's decision poses the question as to the intention of the legislature in providing for publication of the various notices in a newspaper published "in the next nearest town or city" in case there is none "published within the territory described in the petition." It holds them mandatory and necessary to the formation of a de jure school corporation.

Defendants contend the county superintendent acquires jurisdiction "by the filing with him of the petition required under" Code section 276.2, I.C.A., "and his jurisdiction once acquired is not lost by subsequent omission to follow literally and strictly the statutes."

They argue the courts have been liberal in construction of school organization statutes and that the notices in question are "of the informational type rather than the type upon which jurisdiction depends, since jurisdiction is conferred not by the notices, but by filing the petion [*sic*]."

The term "jurisdiction" has been said to be one "in general use, of comprehensive and large import, having different meanings, dependent on the connection in which it is found and the subject matter to which it is directed." 50 C.J.S., Jurisdiction, § 296, pp. 1089, 1090. As applied to courts it is "a term of large and comprehensive import and embraces every kind of judicial action, and hence every movement by a court is necessarily the exercise of jurisdiction. It includes jurisdiction over the subject matter as well as over the person." 14 Am. Jur., Courts, § 160.

It is important to determine in what sense the word is used when we find it in a judicial opinion or in legal argument. Defendants' argument does not do this. As used in Zilske v. Albers, 238 Iowa 1050, 1055, 29 N.W. 2d 189, and other cases cited by defendants referring to administrative, as distinguished from judical proceedings, the word doubtless corresponds roughly to what is termed "jurisdiction of subject matter." If, as in the statutes involved here, some method or form of notice is provided for rendering subsequent proceedings binding upon interested individuals, "jurisdiction" or power to be so obtained is comparable to what in legal proceedings, we call jurisdiction of the person. When "jurisdiction" is mentioned we need often, as here, to consider which kind is meant.

* * * * * * * * * * * * * * * * *

. . . in matters of this kind the distinction made in judicial procedure between jurisdiction of the subject matter and jurisdiction of the person must be kept in mind.

It is true, when the petition was filed in compliance with statute, the county superintendent acquired jurisdiction (or authority) to proceed in the matter. But to retain that jurisdiction, *as to persons affected by the proposed formation of a consolidated district,* the prescribed subsequent notices must be given in substantial compliance with the statute.

Defendants argue that had the statute been followed it would have meant publication "in the Tripoli Leader, the newspaper having the smallest general circulation in the county." They also say: "It would seem that almost any published notice sufficient to advise the public generally such as the notices in this case would be sufficient to sustain this consolidation. As an actual matter of fact, fewer people would have had knowledge if the statutes in question had been literally followed."

Unfortunately for this argument the legislature saw fit to specify the exact manner of selecting the medium of publication. It did not specify publication "in such paper as would reach the greater number of people." Nor did it entrust to the county superintendent any discretion in selecting the medium of publication which that official deemed best suited to the purpose. On the contrary it carefully prescribed that if no newspaper be published *"within* the (described) territory" the notice *shall* be given in one published "in the *next nearest town* or city." And significantly it expressly made the same requirement as to all three notices. (In their reply brief defendants argue the word "shall" in section 276.4 "refers mainly to the time in which certain notice should be given rather than the manner" of giving. Somewhere in the sentence they would have us insert the word "may." We cannot do this.)

These notices were for the benefit, not of specific individuals but of all persons interested, adversely or otherwise, in the project—in the language of Code section 276.5, I.C.A.: "all parties concerned, having due regard for the welfare of adjoining districts."

Possibly the legislature might have left the selection to the official. But certainly had it so intended it would not have given such explicit directions.

We do not deem the notices as merely "informational." They were, in the sense we have endeavored to define, "jurisdictional." Substantial compliance with the statute was a necessary condition precedent to the formation of a de jure school corporation under Code chapter 276, I.C.A., binding on all interested persons.

The cases cited by defendants, properly analyzed, are not in disharmony with our conclusion here. None is directly in point. We do not find there has been any precedent involving the exact question presented. It is essentially one of first impression.

We appreciate (with considerable sympathy) something of the difficulties confronting county superintendents under our present complex and frequently changing school statutes. But we are clear the requirements here were mandatory and necessary to the consummation of the proposed consolidation.

Guides for Class Discussion

1. What did the court mean when it said the question was essentially one of "first impression"?
2. Do you think the court ruled properly? Give reasons.
3. Why was the court so concerned over the matter of "jurisdiction"?

16. *"The courts will not permit minor irregularities, which could not have affected the outcome of an election, to defeat the will of the people"* (p. 5).

STATE v. SCHMIESING,
243 Minn. 11, 66 N.W. (2d) 20 (1954)
(Decided by the Supreme Court of Minnesota)

[This was an action to determine whether an independent school district was legally constituted and had the authority to function as a duly organized school district. Specifically, one point at issue was whether certain alleged irregularities in holding the election for the purpose of putting to a vote the question of the organization into a single district of several districts and parts of other districts, invalidated the election. The lower court held the election valid, and the Supreme Court affirmed the decision of the lower court.]

NELSON, Justice.

This is a proceeding in quo warranto originally commenced in the district court for the county of Traverse with the consent of the attorney general to determine whether Independent Consolidated Joint School District No. 61 of Traverse county and No. 86 of Wilkin county is a lawfully constituted consolidated school district; whether it has authority to function as a duly organized school district; and further whether the respondent individuals named are authorized to act as school board members of said district. . . .

.   .   .   .

Notice of the . . . election was duly and properly posted by the county superintendent of schools pursuant to statute. The county superintendent determines the date with the approval of the survey committee. The call had the approval of the school survey committee based upon its report in its revised form. Although the survey committee in issuing its approval indicated that the superintendent was directed to publish the election notice, this was not necessary in order to comply with the required statutory notice, since § 122.21, as incorporated in § 122.52, requires publication of notice only when a newspaper is published within the proposed consolidated district, and there was no newspaper published within the territory involved. Therefore the order for publication by the survey committee was immaterial to the validity of the election.

The school election of February 20, 1953, was held for the purpose of putting to a vote the reorganization into a new district of districts 14, 27, 36, 41, 44, 56, 60, 17 less section 15, 28 less sections 29 and 32 of Traverse county, and district No. 35 and district No. 10 less sections 9 and 10 of Wilkin county. At this election the proposal for reorganization carried, the vote in the rural areas being 94 in favor of reorganization and 70 opposed, and in the urban area, 82 in favor of reorganization and five opposed. No election was held in three of the rural districts due to a severe snowstorm, inclement weather, and highway conditions in these three districts. Thereafter and on March 2, 1953, the superintendent issued an order reorganizing the territory into one school district to be known as Independent Consolidated Joint School District No. 61 of Traverse county and No. 86, Wilkin county. On April 13, 1953, the individual respondents in this proceeding were duly elected members of the school board of the new school district and thereafter duly qualified.

. . . .

Relators also contend that the following irregularities are sufficient to render the election invalid, viz.: Holding the election in unlawful polling places; irregularities in the appointment of election officials; and violating the statue or the notice of election as to the hours the polls were to be kept open.

Section 122.52, subd. 2, provides:

". . . Wherever possible the election shall be held in the school building of the school districts included in the proposal."

The wording of the statute indicates that an element of discretion in designating the voting place was given to the school survey committee and the county superintendent. There is nothing in the evidence to indicate an abuse of discretion in the choice of the polling places. The evidence discloses that one schoolhouse had been closed for several years and that in prior years homes had been designated and used as polling places. It is well established that an irregularity of this nature, should it be considered such, will not render an election invalid when the change is made in good faith and no one is misled. . . . In the absence of convincing evidence to the contrary, which is lacking here, the presumption of regularity of official acts applies. . . .

In the absence of two other appointed judges, the clerk of the school board in district No. 27 appointed two other persons to act as judges in their stead, and the three then kept the polls open for the required period. Six votes were cast in district No. 27, and these were received, tabulated, and returned which were the votes of all persons who voted in that district.

Relators contend that the mere absence of the officers appointed in the notice of election is an irregularity sufficient to invalidate the election. Nothing appears in the evidence to even remotely indicate that the conduct of those who became the final judges of the election was not fair and honest.

It has been held by this court that, if the election board was completed by the selection of others under color of authority, who might be officers *de facto*, the election is then valid. . . . The important question is whether the election has been honestly and fairly conducted, and if it has, the failure to have present at the election the full number of election officers required by law, either permanently or by reason of temporary absence, is not fatal to the validity of an election. . . .

. . . .

Section 122.52, subd. 2, provides that the judges appointed for each polling place shall be school board members *if they are available.* There is no evidence here on the question of availability. In its absence, again, the presumption must be that the school survey committee and the county superintendent, in an exercise of the discretion given them on availability, made their selection of judges pursuant to statutory requirements. . . .

Section 122.52, subd. 2, provides:

". . . The polls shall be open for at least two hours, and may be open for a longer period, not to exceed 12 hours, if so designated in the posted and published notices."

The notice of election, in this case, required the polls to be open from 4 p.m. to 7 p.m. on February 20, 1953, a period of three hours. The notice complied with the requirement of the statute. The only instances where this requirement was not fulfilled was in those districts where no election was held at all, as hereafter discussed.

The evidence is clear that weather conditions and a severe snowstorm made travel difficult throughout the territory where the election was scheduled and in some parts, according to the testimony, apparently impossible. As a result no election was actually held in districts 28, 44, 56. None came to the polling place to vote in district No. 28. As to district No. 44, there was testimony by a voter to the effect that his failure to vote was due entirely to the storm, and the clerk of the district testified that the polls in that district were not open because of the storm and that no one, to his knowledge, came to vote and was unable to do so. The clerk of district No. 56 testified that her husband and two other men were the only persons who appeared at the polling place which in that instance was open from 4:15 p.m. to 5:45 p.m. There is no testimony that any person appeared prior to opening or after closing for the purpose of voting. These four persons who appeared did not vote, but this was a matter of their own choice based upon the belief that their ballots could not be counted without all of the regularly appointed election judges being present.

It appears from the evidence that six voters who came to the polls did not cast their ballots. However, the canvassed result in the election, disclosed by the return of February 27, 1953, showed:

Total for reorganization 176
Total against reorganization 75

Ten rural school districts were involved in the reorganization plan and recommendations. Seven of these made a return of votes cast at the election. Wherever such votes were cast, counted, and returned no question has been raised that the polls were not open the time required by law. In the other three districts where the polls were not open, it clearly appears from the evidence that the only cause was the stormy weather accompanied by snow and the blocking of highways, a condition over which neither the school survey committee, the superintendent, the election judges, or the voters had any control. The severity appears to have been such that, had the three other polling places been open the full time, only six additional votes would have been cast. It is apparent from the record that the result of the election would not have been changed had every voter who was known to have come to the polls been able to cast his vote.

. . . .

No fraud or illegal practice on the part of election officials has been shown. The failure to open certain polling places as regularly scheduled was due to a severe snowstorm which the evidence quite convincingly establishes was the sole cause. Since the evidence is sufficiently clear that no change in the election would have resulted if all the polling places had been kept open, we conclude that the relators have failed to establish their contention that the election was invalid or to effectively challenge the facts as found by the trial court below, whose findings have the same effect and the same binding force as the verdict of a jury. The trial court found that the school election of February 20, 1953, was not invalid because of the fact that no voters appeared at certain polling places due to a severe snowstorm and blocked roads.

The relators argue that the election could have been called by those charged with that duty under the statute at some other time of the year and thereby severe weather and the possibility of a snowstorm and blocked roads could have been avoided. But, as the trial court stated in its memorandum, "the statute places no restriction of any kind upon the Survey Committee as to the season during which the election should be held."

We are not aware that any such controls are permitted or restrictions exist where free elections are the order of the day. It is the prerogative of the survey committee and the superintendent to exercise their judgment and discretion in that regard, and the courts have no right to interfere with the exercise of that duty to the extent of passing upon their wisdom or lack of it in selecting a certain day in the future for voting. If the statute is otherwise complied with as to election requirements, if good faith has been exercised by the election officials so that thereby no one has been misled, and if the officials have not under the law failed to perform their statutory duties, then the date set will have to stand. . . . If an election is held in fact, it is valid, though there may have been interference as there was here by the elements. The vote may be reduced thereby or the outcome changed, but qualified voters who fail to go to the polls to vote under the circumstances will be bound by the expressed will of those who do. Of course, natural conditions over which man may exercise control may prevent an election in fact, but we think that interference short of that may not be classed as jurisdictional.

This must of necessity be the rule, or there would be no solid ground upon which candidate or voter could stand, for endless confusion and uncertainty would otherwise result. The trial court assigned like reasoning for the inability of either side to produce a case in point.

Guides for Class Discussion

1. What principles of law relating to the legality of elections can be gleaned from this decision?
2. Do you agree with this holding? Why or why not?
3. What did the court say with regard to its role in the matter of elections?
4. Had there been any evidence of fraud, how do you think the court would have held?
5. Compare the decision in this case with the one in *State* v. *Consolidated Independent School District, supra.*

17. ". . . *statutory provisions regulating an election will be treated as mandatory before an election, but as directory afterwards*" (p. 5).

STATE V. INDEPENDENT CONSOLIDATED SCHOOL DISTRICT,
253 Minn. 271, 92 N.W. (2d) 70 (1958)
(Decided by the Supreme Court of Minnesota)

[This was an action brought to test the validity of reorganization of school districts. One of the grounds for so doing was that several irregularities occurred in the election procedure.]

KNUTSON, Justice.

. . . .

It is the contention of relators that publication of the notice in the Hanska Herald was a jurisdictional prerequisite to a valid election. M.S.A. § 122.52, subd. 1, as far as material, reads:

". . . A notice of election shall be given, the question submitted, the election held and the vote canvassed and reported in accordance with the provisions of Minnesota Statutes, section 122.21, for the submission of a similar or like proposal. . . ."

Section 122.21 subd. 1, as far as material here, reads:

". . . such notice shall be published once, at least ten days prior to the date of such meeting or election, in a newspaper, whether it be a legal newspaper or not, if there be one published in said proposed consolidated school district. . . ."

The Hanska Herald is published in the proposed school district. The plain language of this statutory provision requires publication of the notice in the Hanska Herald.

At the outset, we wish to say that it is difficult for us to understand why public officials chargeable with the duty of proceeding according to law, and their legal advisors, choose to ignore the plain requirement of a statute. There is nothing ambiguous about this provision. It should have been a simple matter to follow it. Relators contend that it was not followed for the reason that someone wanted to hold the election on the reorganization before the election could be held on the consolidation of a part of District No. 7 with the Madelia district. The obvious intentional disregard of this plain statutory requirement gives much support to this contention. Respondents' explanation is that it was undesirable to hold an election during the Christmas holidays, but no reason has been advanced why it could not have been held after the holidays. It should also be noted that the election on the consolidation of District

No. 7 with the Madelia district was held during the Christmas holidays. However, courts are reluctant to hold invalid elections even though statutory proceedings have not been followed, unless it clearly appears that they were jurisdictional requirements, where the results show that there has been a free and fair expression of the voters. In In re Order of Sammons, County Superintendent of Schools, 242 Minn. 345, 349, 65 N.W.2d 198, 202, we said:

"It is the general rule that, *before an election is held,* statutory provisions regulating the conduct of the election will usually be treated as mandatory and their observance may be insisted upon and enforced. *After an election has been held,* the statutory regulations are generally construed as directory and such rule of construction is in accord with the policy of this state, which from its beginning has been that, in the absence of fraud or bad faith or constitutional violation, an election which has resulted in a fair and free expression of the will of the legal voters upon the merits will not be invalidated because of a departure from the statutory regulations governing the conduct of the election except in those cases where the legislature has clearly and unequivocally expressed an intent that a specific statutory provision is an essential jurisdictional prerequisite and that a departure therefrom shall have the drastic consequence of invalidity."

The application of the above rule is particularly apropos where it appears that failure to comply with a statutory requirement could not have affected the result of the election. Here, there were 779 eligible voters. Of these, 502 were in the rural areas and 277 in the urban area. 464 of the 502 voters in the rural area voted at the election; 38 did not vote; 290 voted in favor and 174 against the reorganization; hence it carried in the rural area by 116 votes. In the urban area, 241 of the 277 eligible voters cast their votes. Of these, 236 were in favor and 5 against; 36 eligible voters did not vote; consequently the proposition carried in the urban area by 231 votes. Even if all 38 rural voters and all 36 urban voters who failed to vote had cast their votes against the proposition, it still would have carried. In view of this fact, we hold that failure to publish the notice in the Hanska Herald could not possibly have affected the results of the election. While that fact does not excuse willful failure to follow the statute, under the circumstances of this case we are inclined to hold that it was not such an irregularity as would vitiate the election. While so doing, we wish to caution those chargeable with the conduct of such elections that in other cases, where it does not so clearly appear that failure to follow the statute has not affected the outcome, a deliberate failure to follow a statutory requirement as clear as this one may well be fatal. Where the meaning of the statute is unambiguous, there is no excuse for ignoring it.

Was the notice sufficiently clear to apprise the voters of the territory involved in the reorganization and the place where the balloting was to be conducted? The notice read as follows:

"Notice is hereby given that a special election in school districts Nos. 7, 38, 53, 54, 31, 67, 75, and 81 in Brown County, Minnesota, will be held at school house on the 20th day of December 1956, from 1:00 o'clock p.m. to 4:00 o'clock p.m., for the following purposes: Shall school districts Nos. 7, 38, 53, 54, 31, 67, 75, 81 and part of District 28 be merged to form one district as set forth in the final report of the Brown County Survey Committee?"

The argument is that, inasmuch as the territory is inaccurately described and the place of election is "held at school house," the voters could not know where the voting would take place.

What we have said above with respect to publication of the notice applies equally to the designation of the place of voting. So large a proportion of eligible voters actually cast their votes that it can hardly be said that they were misled as to the place of voting. Even if a few were misled, it could have not changed the result, for as we have shown above, even if all eligible voters who did not vote had cast their votes against the proposition, the result would have been the same.

With respect to the area to be included in the reorganized district, the objection is that the portion of the notice which reads "part of District 28" was incorrect. While this description is not as complete as it might have been, we are convinced that the voters were well aware of the area to be included. This was the third election held. The area was the same as that previously rejected, with the exception of that part of Watonwan County District No. 49 attached in Brown County which, prior to the third election, had been consolidated with the Madelia district. The notice states that the reorganized district is to be formed "as set forth in the final report of the Brown County Survey Committee." This report describes the area in District No. 28 which is to be included. Under these circumstances, we are of the opinion that the notice was not so inaccurate as to invalidate the election.

Guides for Class Discussion

1. Compare this decision with the decision in *State v. Consolidated Independent School District, supra.* Can you reconcile the two?

2. Compare this decision with the one in *State v. Schmiesing, supra.*

3. Do you agree with the court's reasoning? Give reasons.

18. *"Since school districts are but parts of the machinery employed in carrying out the educational policies of the state, the
legislature, in addition to creating school districts, may abolish
them, or alter their boundaries as public policy may dictate"* (p. 5).

PEOPLE v. DEATHERAGE,
401 Ill. 25, 81 N.E. (2d) 581 (1948)
(Decided by the Supreme Court of Illinois)

[This action was brought to test the validity of the organization of a school district and the right of defendants to hold office.
Involved in the case was the question of the legality of the
statute under which the district was organized. The lower court
ruled for the   defendant, and the court, here, affirmed the decision of the lower court. In arriving at its decision, the court
considered the authority of the legislature to create, abolish,
or to alter the boundaries of school districts.]

CRAMPTON, Justice.

.   .   .   .

We must first ascertain whether this court has the duty and the
power to determine whether a specific school system is thorough and
efficient. Where issues before this court involve the constitutionality of
statutes permitting the creation of school districts, the court is necessarily
limited in decision to a narrow field. This is true because of the inherent
power of the legislature and section 1 of article VIII of the constitution.
The section simply operates as a mandate to the legislature to exercise its
inherent power to carry out a primary, obligatory concept of our system
of government, i.e., the children of the State are entitled to a good
common-school education, in public schools, and at public expense. Prior
decisions of this court have held the section to also place upon the
legislature two limitations when implementing that concept: the schools
established, i.e., the system, must be free and must be open to all without
discrimination. . . .

This court has also been consistent in holding that the question of
the efficiency and thoroughness of the school system established by
legislative permission is one solely for the legislature to answer and
that the courts lack power to intrude. . . . In Fiedler v. Eckfeldt, 335
Ill. 11, 166 N.E. 504, 509, we said, it is not for the court to determine
if the system is the best which could be brought forth. School problems are essentially practical ones,—what is best cannot be easily
answered. . . . ". . . Even if the legislative intent might be thought

crude or unwise and the law unjust or oppressive, errors of legislation are not subject to judicial review unless they exceed some limitation imposed by the constitution. Within those limitations the legislative power is supreme, and judicial power cannot interfere with it."

A community unit school district, like any other school district established under enabling legislation, is entirely subject to the will of the legislature thereafter. With or without the consent of the inhabitants of a school district, over their protests, even without notice or hearing, the State may take the school facilities in the district, without giving compensation therefor, and vest them in other districts or agencies. The State may hold or manage the facilities directly or indirectly. The area of the district may be contracted or expanded, it may be divided, united in whole or in part with another district, and the district may be abolished. All this at the will of the legislature. The "property of the school district" is a phrase which is misleading. The district owns no property, all school facilities, such as grounds, buildings, equipment, etc., being in fact and law the property of the State and subject to the legislative will. . . .

. . . .

We take judicial notice of the fact that the whole area of the State has been divided into school districts. Therefore the territory described in the petition for the organization of the Waverly Community Unit School District No. 6 must have included the territories of several whole school districts. No evidence was heard in this case in the court below, and we cannot tell from the record whether the organization of the Waverly district resulted in the fractioning of one or more underlying districts. In any event, the mere fact of a school district being fractioned when a community unit school district is organized, does not *ipso facto* establish that the school system, within the emasculated district, lacks efficiency and thoroughness.

In People ex rel. Russell v. Graham, 301 Ill. 446, 134 N.E. 57, the constitutionality of the act enabling the establishment of community consolidated school districts was under attack. . . . It was charged the act did not provide a thorough and efficient system of free schools, so all the children of the State may receive a good common-school education. Therein we held, 301 Ill. at page 451, 134 N.E. at page 60, "The wisdom or justice of such legislation is not a question for the courts. The courts are concerned only with the question of the legislative power to enact it." . . .

Counsel endeavor to involve the act under consideration with section 1 of article VIII of the constitution on the following theory: the thoroughness and efficiency of the system of free schools must redound to the benefit of *all* children of the State, to the extent they may receive a good common-school education. This is predicated upon the proposition that the residents and voters of the underlying districts have certain vested property rights therein which cannot rightfully be de-

stroyed or impaired by the absorption of whole, or portions of underlying districts. Less than all of the children will be served, it is
said, whose parents happen to live in that portion of a fractioned district which is not taken into the petition for the organization of the *first*
community unit school district. This viewpoint rests upon the presumed
deprivation of adequate school facilities claimed as a vested property
right. Our holding in the *Camargo case* that all school facilities are the
property of the State, subject to the will of the legislature in effectuating
the policy adopted in order to carry out the constitutional mandate,
destroys the contention.

.   .   .   .

It is further contended the act deprives those voters residing in the
territory of an existing district, which is not taken into the new community unit school district, of their right to vote on the proposition
of organizing the unit district contrary to section 18 of article II of
the constitution; their standpoint being that such election cannot be
free and equal. We concede such persons would have a great personal
interest in such election, either from the standpoint of desiring all their
district taken in or all not taken. The mandate of section 18 of article
II covers only those who are qualified voters in the particular election.
It does not guarantee that every person with a patent interest in the
outcome of a school election has, because of that interest, a right to
vote therein. The legislature possessing all power to legislate in reference to public school matters, limited only by the stated limitations
found in section 1 of article VIII of the constitution, no resident of a
school district has an inherent right of franchise insofar as school
elections are concerned. His right to vote therein is purely a permissive
one bestowed by legislative grace in furtherance of the policy of the
legislature. The bestowal of the power to organize a school district,
either by petition or by election, bestows only a privilege as distinguished
from a right. . . .

.   .   .   .

The legislature has always, as a matter of policy, left to the resident
voters the settlement of all questions involving school district territory.
They acted to determine such questions either through the mode of
petitioned elections or by petitions to the appropriate public official or
officials clothed by law with the power to annex or detach territory;
the legislative theory, of course, being that at the time of or subsequent
to the organization of a school district there necessarily would arise
certain territorial inequities involving matters of population, valuations
of property for taxation, compactness and contiguity, and other matters.
The resident voters of the particular territory are the delegated agents
of the legislature to administer the enabling legislation, thereby implementing the legislative intent to obey the constitutional mandate of
insuring an efficient and thorough common schooling for all the children
of the State via free public schools, open to all without discrimination.

Those voters, in a practical sense, become administrative functionaries to administer the law. Whenever they utilize the delegated administrative power and authority to impair the complementary nature of the two factors of classification, and thereby disturb the balance between pupil load and tax income to an extent which renders the district inefficient and lacking thoroughness from the scholastic standpoint, those voters have violated the trust placed in them by the legislature. Such improper use of that power and authority simply entails a plea to the legislature for remedial action. The courts cannot act to give relief from such violations of administrative functions, unless such violations fall within the scope of constitutional limitations. . . .

. . . .

Lastly, our attention is directed to section 20 of article II of the State constitution: "A frequent recurrence to the fundamental principles of civil government is absolutely necessary to preserve the blessings of liberty." This court is ever mindful of that admonition. In this case we have adhered to the fundamental principle of the three main grand divisions of government, the legislative, the administrative and the judicial, by refusing to intrude into the legislative area and undertake to say what is a thorough and efficient system of free schools for the common schooling of all the children of the State.

The argument presented under this point stresses the inability of all the voters of a school district, intended for loss of some territory, to vote on the question of the organization of the community unit school district. Such is said to be an impairment of their liberties, i.e., the use and enjoyment of an existing, excellent school system. That use and enjoyment, when regarded as a liberty, presupposes the existence of a right, either created, or guaranteed by, the State constitution. Elsewhere in this opinion we have shown the utter absence, under the constitution, of any right in a particular segment of the population to the continued enjoyment of a particular school system, contrary to the will of the legislature. The people of the State have given to the legislature all power over the public schools and school system, subject only to the two limitations in section 1 of article VIII.

Judgment affirmed.

Guides for Class Discussion

1. What did the court say with respect to the authority of the judicial department of government over the creation of school districts?

2. What line of reasoning did the court follow in arriving at its decision?

3. What limits did the court place on the legislature's authority to create school districts?

4. What did the court say about the ownership of school property?

5. What right do the inhabitants of a district have to object if the legislature alters the boundaries of the district? Must they give their consent?

6. Compare this decision with *Associated Schools* v. *School District, supra.*

19. *"When district boundaries are changed, the legislature may dispose of property and of pre-existing assets and liabilities in such manner as may be deemed reasonable and just"* (p. 5).

ATTORNEY GENERAL v. LOWREY,
131 Mich. 639, 92 N.W. 289 (1902)
(Decided by the Supreme Court of Michigan)

[In this action, inquiring into the right of certain school officers to hold office, it was contended that the district was created illegally. Among other things, it was argued that the statute that provided for the allocation of district assets when boundary lines are changed was illegal.]

HOOKER, C. J.

.   .   .   .

. . . The school district is a state agency. Moreover, it is of legislative creation. It is true that it was provided for in obedience to a constitutional requirement; and whatever we may think of the right of the district to administer in a local way the affairs of the district, under the constitution, we cannot doubt that such management must be in conformity to the provisions of such laws of a general character as may from time to time be passed, and that the property of the district is in no sense private property, but is public property devoted to the purposes of the state, for the general good, just as almshouses and courthouses are, although confided to local management, and applied to uses which are in a sense local, though in another sense general.

.   .   .   .

Among the above points, our attention is naturally attracted to "c," wherein it is stated that the territory excluded is deprived of any share of the public property. It does not seem to be denied that the legislature may change the boundaries of districts. That has been too often done to admit of question. Numerous school districts have lost territory through city charters, and the case of Keweenaw Ass'n v. School Dist. No. 1, 98 Mich. 437, 57 N. W. 404, is conclusive upon the point. . . . The authority of the legislature to change the boundaries of counties, townships, and school districts does not necessarily involve the obligation to reimburse the portion deprived of the use of the public property. Frequently such laws contain provisions for the purpose, but it is not necessary. The property is public property, held and used for the purposes of the state, which may, in the absence of constitutional prohibition, make such disposition of it as it sees fit. . . .

Whatever we may think of the justice of this act (and we cannot say that the situation was not fully known and discussed by the legislature), we cannot doubt the legislative authority to change these districts, and provide for the disposal of their property and payment of their debts, as was done in this case. The law is said to fix the site of a school building. This is not usual, but we are not convinced that it is beyond the power of the legislature to locate its schoolhouses, courthouses, and almshouses. No authority is cited to the contrary, and, without deciding the question, we may say that the sites alluded to had already been located, and one built upon by the districts. In saying that these should be deemed to be, respectively, a schoolhouse site, and the central schoolhouse for the new district, the legislature, if it had not the power to fix beyond revocation such sites, can easily be held to have made a provision which was directory merely; and, whatever we may think of their power in the premises, no one would claim that it was designed to forbid future action by the board, and we might safely eliminate the provision, if necessary to sustain the act, in accordance with a common and well-understood rule.

But it is said that some of the territory was left out of the new district, and that the legislature fixed definitely what should be done with it, and appointed the officers who should attach it to new districts. If this opinion is correct upon the first point discussed, it cannot be doubted that the legislature might itself have attached this territory to specific districts. This it did not do, but attempted to confide the subject to the township school inspectors. This was the board authorized to deal with such questions, and had been elected by the township for such purposes. This cannot be said to be an appointment by the legislature. . . .

Guides for Class Discussion

1. Compare this case with *Board of Education of Barker District* v. *Board of Education of Valley District, infra.*
2. Do you think this decision is equitable? Give reasons.
3. What assurance is there that the general principle of law enunciated here will not lead to injustice on occasion?
4. If injustice should result what recourse does an aggrieved party have?

20. ". . . *the transfer of property from one district to another is not a violation of rights guaranteed by the federal constitution*" (p. 5).

STATE v. BROOKS,
249 S. W. 73 (Mo.) (1923)
(Decided by the Supreme Court of Missouri)

[This was an action brought to oust certain school directors from office. It was contended that the district was without existence because it was unlawfully organized. One contention was that the act under which the district was organized was unconstitutional because it resulted in transferring funds of one specific district to the consolidated district without the consent of the voters of that district.]

SMALL, C. . . .

This is an information exhibited by the prosecuting attorney of Nodaway county at the relation of R. I. Bilby, as a taxpayer, freeholder, and voter residing in school district No. 104 of said county. Its purpose, as alleged by relator, is to oust the defendants, respondents herein, from the pretended office of school directors of the pretended consolidated school district No. 102, made up of the pretended consolidation of school districts Nos. 74, 75, 101, 102, 103, 104, 105, and 109, all located within said county, for the reason that said pretended consolidated school district No. 102 was unlawfully organized because the plats and notices required by law were insufficient within the meaning of the statute (Laws of 1913 p. 721, now section 11259, R. S. 1919); and for the further reason that the law providing for such consolidation is unconstitutional.

The issues were joined and the evidence heard (which will be referred to in the opinion), and the court on February 17, 1922, rendered its decree sustaining the validity of the organization of said consolidated school district No. 102.

Motion for new trial being overruled, relator duly appealed to this court.

The first contention of the relator is: That the notices of the election to be held to vote on the proposition of forming said consolidated school district were insufficient, because the law (section 11259, R. S. 1919) requiring 10 notices of said election to be posted was not complied with, in that "three of the notices so posted omitted school district No. 109, and one of said notices omitted districts Nos. 103 and 109."

. . . .

We hold therefore, that there was substantial evidence that all districts to be consolidated were mentioned in at least ten of the notices posted. The finding of the lower court to that effect is therefore conclusive upon us. State ex rel. Roberts v. Stephens (Mo. Sup.) 243 S. W. 89.

It is also contended that the notices were not signed by the county superintendent of public schools of Nodaway county. While it is true the name of the superintendent is apparently not now visible on a number of the notices introduced in evidence, the superintendent testified in the case for respondents that all the notices were signed by him before being posted. . . .

. . . .

The contention that the act consolidating school districts, as applied to this case, is unconstitutional because one of the districts, No. 104, in which relator lived, had $585.23 in its treasury, which was transferred to the consolidated district without the consent of the vote of the people of that district, cannot be sustained. School districts and their property are creatures of the state which may be created and abolished at will by the Legislature, and *no provision of the Constitution, either state or federal, is violated by consolidating any such school district and its property with others to form a new or consolidated district.* [Emphasis added.] State ex rel. Richart v. Stouffer, 197 S. W. 248 (this court); State ex inf. Wright v. Morgan, 268 Mo. 265, 187 S. W. 54; State ex rel. v. Hill, 152 Mo. 238, 53 S. W. 1062; State ex rel. v. Jones, 266 Mo. 198, 181 S. W. 50.

Finding no error, the judgment below is affirmed.

Guides for Class Discussion

1. Compare this case with *In re School Committee of North Smithfield, infra* and *Ross* v. *Adams Mills Rural School District, infra.*
2. On what ground did the court justify its holding that the act was constitutional?
3. Are you in agreement with the court's ruling? Give reasons.

21. *". . . [the] transfer of property [from one district to another] is not in violation of a contract because no contractual relation exists between the state and its school districts"* (p. 5).

IN RE SCHOOL COMMITTEE OF NORTH SMITHFIELD,
26 R. I. 164, 58 A. 628 (1904)
(Decided by the Supreme Court of Rhode Island)

[This was an application for the appointment of a commission to appraise property of the school district of North Smithfield which, under an act abolishing the district, had become vested in the town. A taxpayer and trustee objected to the proceedings claiming that the act was unconstitutional because, among other things, it deprived citizens of property without due process of law, and because it impaired the obligations of contracts.]

STINESS, C. J. . . .

. . . .

It is a sufficient answer to the first objection that the prohibition of the Constitution applies only to the taking of private property for public use, and the act in question takes no property of the objector or of any other individual. School districts and towns are corporations for public purposes. Taxpayers have no private title or interest in the property held by such corporations. That public property may be taken for public use is too obvious for argument. In fact, however, the law in question takes no property at all, in the sense in which the term is used in the condemnation of property to public use. It is already school property. It is to be devoted to no new use. The custody, control, and nominal title of the property is transferred from the school district to the town for the same public use. The law therefore affects no private right of property.

The other objections—that the law impairs the obligation of a contract, that it vests the property in the town without its consent, and that it does not provide for a jury trial—may be considered together.

The duties of a school district are obligations imposed, not a contract. Districts and towns undertake to provide for the education of children, not by force of any agreement, but as a duty required of them by law, like the duty to keep highways in repair. The extent, control, and change of this duty is under the direction of the Legislature. The consent of the municipal corporation is not required. As said by Mr. Justice Clifford in Mt. Pleasant v. Beckwith, 100 U. S. 514, 25 L. Ed. 699: "Power exists here in the Legislature not only to fix the boundaries of such a municipality when incorporated, but to enlarge or diminish the same subsequently, without the consent of the residents, by annexation or set-off, unless restrained by the Constitution, even against the remonstrance of every property holder and voter within the limits of the original municipality. Property set off or annexed may be benefited or burdened by the change, and the liability of the residents to taxation may be increased or diminished; but the question, in every case, is entirely within the control of the Legislature, and, if no provision is made, everyone must submit to the will of the state, as expressed through the legislative department." . . . In Rawson v. Spencer, 113 Mass. 40, the constitutionality of a statute almost identical with the one before us, in its main provision, was fully considered. In that case the town gave implied assent by appointing appraisers, but assent was not necessary, as the statute was peremptory and made no provision for assent. The court held that the statute was not unconstitutional upon the grounds that district property was taken without compensation, that the taxes to be imposed were not proportional, or that the act impaired the obligation of contracts. The decision was based upon the principle that the law was a legitimate exercise of the power by which the Legislature may require the performance of public duties by different municipal or political agencies at its discretion. The court said: "School districts were indeed quasi corporations, with the power to hold property, to raise money by taxation for the support of schools, and with certain defined duties. But they were public and political as distinguished from private corporations, and their rights and powers were held at the will of the Legislature, to be modified or abolished as public welfare might require. The property held by them for public use was subject to such disposition in the promotion of the objects for which it was held as the supreme legislative power might see fit to make."

  . . . .

We are of opinion that the act is not unconstitutional, and the case is remitted to the common pleas division for further proceedings.

Guides for Class Discussion

1. How did the court justify its holding that the act in question did not impair the obligation of contracts? Do you agree?
2. Do you think courts today would agree with this decision?
3. What did the court say about the nature of school districts?
4. What is the significance of the fact the court distinguished between public and private property?

22. ". . . *the transfer of property from district to district by annexation of territory [does not] violate the due-process-of-law clause of the Fourteenth Amendment*" (p. 5).

Ross v. Adams Mills Rural School District,
113 Ohio St. 466, 149 N.E. 634 (1925)
(Decided by the Supreme Court of Ohio)

[This was an action against the board of education of the Adams Mills Rural School District. The essential facts of the case are that a rural school district containing two villages and adjacent territory had caused a new school building to be erected and paid for as a result of the issuance of bonds. Of the total amount, $96,000 were outstanding and unpaid at the time when part of the district was transferred to the Adams Mills Rural District. It should be noted that the building in question was not in the territory transferred to the Adams Mills district. This transfer took place without any action on the part of the board of education or the taxpayers of the district. Later the county board of education ordered that $25,000 of the bonds should be paid by this district. Objection was made to this ruling by the Adams Mills district, but the county auditor, together with the county auditor of an adjacent county in which part of the property was located, levied the tax upon all the property in the district. This action was brought to enjoin the levying and collection of the tax to pay such bonds.]

MATTHIAS, J. . . .

· ·

It seems to be the clear purpose and intent of the provisions of section 4692, General Code, to require that any of the indebtedness of the district from which territory is transferred shall be apportioned between the districts from which and to which such territory is transferred. Indeed, it is impossible to make that provision of the statute effective if not so interpreted and applied.

When such division was made the indebtedness became the indebtedness of the Adams Mills district and of the Jefferson district, as apportioned. Under the provisions of section 4692, General Code, the "legal title of the property of the board of education shall become vested in the board of education of the school district to which such property is transferred," and, when an equitable division of the indebtedness was made, all the property in each district became liable for its respective proportion thereof. There is no statutory provision which would authorize a tax levied upon only a portion of a district or subdivision, and no method has been prescribed, and none has been suggested, whereby that could be done. It would be contrary to the provisions of all tax levying and tax limitation statutes. In accordance with the familiar principles of statutory construction, section 4692, General Code, will be so construed as to make it a valid enactment for all purposes, and proceedings thereunder will, if possible, be so construed as to accomplish a valid result. Just as legislation enacted subsequent to the issuance of bonds that would remove a portion of the security thereof, and thereby impair the obligation of contract, would be invalid as against the holders of said bonds so also would a proceeding under this statute which undertook to transfer a portion of the district be a nullity against holders of the bonds, if it did not provide for the apportionment of the indebtedness and payment of the bonds as contemplated in the original proceeding for the issuance thereof, as required by the constitutional and statutory provisions heretofore referred to.

The contention that such statutory provision is violative of the due process clause of the federal Constitution has been considered in numerous cases and decided adversely thereto. In Hunter v. City of Pittsburgh, 207 U. S. 161, 28 S. Ct. 40, 52 L. Ed. 151, it was held:

"There is no contract, within the meaning of the contract clause of the Federal Constitution, between a municipality and its citizens and taxpayers that the latter shall be taxed only for the uses of that corporation and not for the uses of any like corporation with which it may be consolidated."

The language of Justice Moody, who rendered the opinion of the court, is pertinent here. After referring to the powers conferred upon municipal corporations and their status as political subdivisions of the state, he said, at page 178 (28 S. Ct. 46):

"The State, therefore, at its pleasure may modify or withdraw all such powers, may take without compensation such property, hold it itself, or vest it in other agencies, expand or contract the territorial area, unite the whole or a part of it with another municipality, repeal the charter and destroy the corporation. . . . Although the inhabitants and property owners may by such changes suffer inconvenience, and their property may be lessened in value by the burden of increased taxation, or for any other reason, they have no right by contract or otherwise in the unaltered or continued existence of the corporation or its powers, and there is nothing in the federal Constitution which protects them from these injurious consequences."

.   .   .   .

In the case of Mount Pleasant v. Beckwith, 100 U.S. 514, 25 L. Ed. 699, where it appears that certain municipalities were legislated out of existence, and their territory was by an act of the Legislature brought within the city of Racine, Wis., the court held:

"Where a municipal corporation is legislated out of existence and its territory annexed to other corporations, the latter, unless the Legislature otherwise provides, become entitled to all its property and immunities, and severally liable for a proportionate share of all its then subsisting legal debts, and vested with its power to raise revenue wherewith to pay them by levying taxes upon the property transferred and the persons residing thereon."

.   .   .   .

In the case of State ex rel. v. Cincinnati, 52 Ohio St. 419, 40 N. E. 508, 27 L. R. A. 737, the constitutionality of an act authorizing a city to annex contiguous territory was challenged, and was upheld by this court. It was there held in the syllabus that it is not a valid objection to a statute, or to an annexation under it, that a municipal corporation may be so annexed without the consent of its constituted authorities or inhabitants; nor that the taxable property therein will become subject to taxation for the payment of previously incurred indebtedness of the city to which the annexation is made.

In other jurisdictions the same principle has been applied in cases of consolidation of school districts and of detachment of territory from one school district and its attachment to another. Attorney General of Michigan ex rel. Kies v. Lowrey, 199 U.S. 233, 26 S. Ct. 27, 50 L. Ed. 167; Grout v. Illingworth, Treas., 131 Iowa 281, 108 N. W. 528; Gerhardt v. Yorktown Independent School Dist. (Tex. Civ. App.) 252 S. W. 197; State ex rel. Bilby v. Brooks (Mo. Sup.) 249 S. W. 73. The case last cited seems especially applicable because of the similarity of the legislation under consideration. It was there held that school districts and their property are creatures of the state which may be created and abolished at will by the Legislature. Hence that no provision of the Constitution was violated in providing for consolidation of school districts, even when applied to a district which had a surplus in its treasury which was transferred to the consolidated district.

.   .   .   .

It is well stated in the case of Kneale v. Jennings, 111 Ohio St. 637, 645, 146 N. E. 87, 89, that the "arranging of districts is an administrative matter. The property owner pays taxes for the schools of his district, not because of what the board may do as regards territorial boundaries, but because of a direct requirement of the Constitution."

The facts disclosed would not warrant the conclusion that the county board had abused its discretion in the matter of the division of indebtedness. It follows that the levy made upon property in the Adams Mills district to pay the proportion of the bonded indebtedness of the territory detached from the Jefferson district and transferred to the Adams Mills district, in accordance with the apportionment made by the county board of education, was a valid levy, and that the proceeds thereof must be applied to the discharge of the bonds apportioned to that district as an equitable share of the indebtedness of the territory which was transferred to and became a part of the Adams Mills district.

The judgment of the Court of Appeals in the error proceeding is therefore affirmed, and in the original action in mandamus instituted in this court the demurrer to the petition is overruled and the writ allowed.

Guides for Class Discussion

1. Do you think the court's decision was equitable? Give reasons.
2. What is meant by the due-process-of-law clause?
3. Had there been no statute governing the matter, what rule would the court have undoubtedly followed?
4. Compare this case with *State* v. *Brooks, supra.*

23. *"In case there is no statute governing the disposition of property or the apportionment of debts upon the alteration of school district boundaries, the general rule adopted by the courts is that the property belongs to the district in which it is finally located and each district is liable for the debts it contracted before the change"* (p. 5).

BOARD OF EDUCATION OF BARKER DISTRICT V.
BOARD OF EDUCATION OF VALLEY DISTRICT,
30 W. Va. 424, 4 S.E. 640 (1887)
(Decided by the Supreme Court of Appeals of West Virginia)

[In 1881 the Valley District was created out of territory in the Barker District. When the Valley District refused to pay any part of the indebtedness of the original Barker District, the Barker District brought this action to collect, from the Valley District, its proportionate share of the indebtedness.]

JOHNSON, P. J. . . .

.   .   .   .

Counsel on both sides have entirely misconceived the true question involved in this controversy, and no authority has been cited on that question. The true question is, if there was not by the power that made the division of the district any apportionment of the debts owed by the old district, whether any suit or action will lie to compel the new district to pay any part of the old debt. Corporations of the kind here designated "school-districts" are properly denominated public corporations, for the reason that they are but parts of the machinery employed in carrying on the affairs of the state; and it is well-settled law that the charters under which such corporations are created, may be changed, modified, or repealed, as the exigencies of the public service or the public welfare may demand. . . .

Such corporations are composed of all the inhabitants of the territory included in the political organization; and the attribute of individuality is conferred on the entire mass of such residents, and it may be modified or taken away at the mere will of the legislature, according to its own views of public convenience, and without any necessity for the consent of those composing the body politic. . . . Public duties are required of such corporations as a part of the machinery of the state, and, in order that they may be able to perform their duties, they are invested with certain corporate powers; but their functions are wholly of a public nature, and they are at all times subject to the will of the legislature, unless restricted by the constitution. . . .

But upon the division of an old public corporation, and the creation of a new one out of a part of its inhabitants and territory, the legislature may provide for an equitable appropriation or division of the corporate property, and impose upon the new corporation, or upon the people and territory thus disannexed, the obligation to pay an equitable proportion of the corporate debt. . . .

In *Bristol* v. *New Chester*, 3 N. H. 524 . . . RICHARDSON, C. J. said: "The power to divide towns is strictly legislative, and the power to prescribe the rule by which a division of the property of the old town shall be made is incident to the power to divide the territory, and is in its nature purely legislative. No general rule can be prescribed by which an equal and just division, in such cases, can be made. Such a division must be founded upon the circumstances of each particular case."

In the case cited from 14 Conn. *supra*, WILLIAMS, C. J., said: "The legislature, upon the division of towns and school societies, have always exercised the power, so far as we are informed, of making an equitable arrangement as to the common property and common burdens, and unless this power is taken away by the constitution it must exist as before. . . . If the right remains in the legislature of taking away from such corporations a portion of their inhabitants for whose use the funds were given, it would seem to follow that they must have a right to apportion these in such a manner as to do equal justice to all concerned; always taking care not to violate the intent of a donor thereby, which would not be allowed, even to legislative authority." Where the legislature does not prescribe any regulations for any apportionment of the property, or that the new corporation shall pay any portion of the debt of the old, the old corporation will hold all the corporate property within her new limits, and be entitled to all the claims owing to the old corporation, and is responsible for all the debts of the corporation existing before and at the time of the division, and the new corporation will hold all the corporate property falling within her boundaries, to which the old corporation will have no claim. . . . *Town of Depere* v. *Town of Bellevue,* 31 Wis. 120. In the last-named case it was held that if a part of the territory and inhabitants of a town are separated from it by annexation to another, or by the creation of a new corporation, the remaining part of the town, or the former corporation, retains all its property and francises, and *remains subject to all its obligations*, unless some express provision to the contrary is made by the act authorizing the separation.

In *Laramie Co.* v. *Albany Co.*, 92 U. S. 307, . . . the very able opinion of Mr. Justice CLIFFORD shows the correctness of the several propositions we have announced. In that case it was held, unless the constitution of a state or the organic law of a territory otherwise prescribes, the legislature has the power to diminish or enlarge the area of a county whenever the public convenience or necessity requires; and that where the legislature of Wyoming territory organized two new counties, and included in their limits a part of the territory of an existing county, but made no provision for apportioning debts or liabilities, that the old county, being solely responsible for the debts and liabilities it had previously incurred, had, on discharging them, no claim on the new counties for contribution.

Where a municipal corporation is legislated out of existence, and its territory annexed to other corporations, it has been held that unless the legislature otherwise provides, these other corporations become entitled to all its property and immunities, and are severally liable for a proportionate share of all its then subsisting legal debts, and vested with its power to raise revenue wherewith to pay them, by levying taxes upon the property transferred, and the persons residing thereon, and that the remedy of the creditors of the extinguished corporation is in equity against the corporations succeeding to its property and powers. . . .

.   .   .   .

From what we have said, the power exercised in the division of public corporations being purely legislative, and the power to prescribe the rule by which the property of the corporation shall be divided, and its debts apportioned, being incident to the power to devide the territory, must also be strictly legislative. The courts have no authority over the subject, and can only construe the act of the legislature and see that the legislative will is carried into effect. . . .

.   .   .   .

. . . When the legislature passed the statute it conferred on the county court the same power to divide districts as it possessed itself, and the incident to that power went with it to make provision for apportionment of the property owned by the district, and also whether the new district should pay any part of the old debt, and, if so, how much.

As the court was silent on this subject when the division was made, it follows that the old district of Barker held all the corporate property within its limits, was entitled to collect, and appropriate to its corporate use, all claims due the district, and was bound for all the existing indebtedness of the district. The new district of Valley was entitled to hold all the corporate property of the old district which on the division fell within its bounds, and was not liable for any of the indebtedness of the old district and if Barker district had paid all of the indebtedness of the district existing at the time of division, it has no claim against Valley district for contribution. The decree of the circuit court is reversed, and the bill dismissed.

GREEN, SNYDER, and WOODS, JJ., concurred.

Guides for Class Discussion

1. Are there any restrictions upon the power of the legislature to divide the property and assets of a district from which it detaches territory to be annexed to another?
2. Do you think the court's decision was equitable? Give reasons.
3. What was the line of reasoning the court followed in arriving at its decision?
4. What rule did the court lay down for apportioning the assets and liabilities of a school district that goes out of existence by virtue of the fact various parts of it are annexed to other districts? Is this a fair rule?
5. It will be noted that this case was decided in 1887. Do you think the courts today would accept it as precedent?

24. *"Where a district goes out of existence by annexation to another district . . . the rule is that the subsisting district is entitled to the property and funds and answerable for the debts of the original district"* (p. 6).

WALKER V. BENNETT,
125 S.C. 389, 118 S.E. 779 (1923)
(Decided by the Supreme Court of South Carolina)

[This was an action to restrain the defendants of a newly-consolidated school district from issuing and selling bonds in the amount of $300,000. This action, instituted by plaintiffs, questioned the constitutionality of the law under which the consolidation was formed. Primarily, they contended that, if the outstanding bonded indebtedness of the school district of which they were a member—in the amount of $24,000—continued to be the debt of the school district after the consolidation, the proposed issue of bonds would exceed the constitutional debt limit, so far as the district in question was concerned. In arriving at its decision the court found it necessary to discuss the question of what happens

to the property, funds, and debts of a district that becomes a part
of a new district.]

COTHRAN, J. . . .

.   .   .   .

When the consolidation district was formed, the inevitable result
of the formation was to destroy the existence of the five constituent
school districts in so far as owning separate property and owing
separate debts was concerned. The purpose of the act was to unite the
territory under one school management, which necessarily required that
management to exercise control of all the properties of the constituent
districts and make the consolidated district the unit for the purpose
of owning property, holding assets, paying liabilities and providing
unified system of instruction. . . .

.   .   .   .

In District of Columbia v. Cluss, 103 U. S. 705, 26 L. Ed. 455, it
was held that, where an act uniting a school district into a municipal
corporation was passed, the new corporation succeeded to the property
of the former school district and also succeeded to its liabilities.

A leading case upon the principle under consideration is Town of
Mount Pleasant v. Beckwith, 100 U. S. 514, 25 L. Ed. 699. In the
syllabus it is said:

"Where one town is merged in two others by a legislative act, unless
the Legislature regulate the rights and duties of the two latter, they
succeed to all the public property and immunities of the extinguished
municipality, and they become liable for all the debts previously contracted by it."

In this case the principle was applied to the consolidation of municipalities, but *the same principle applies to the consolidation of school
districts*. [Emphasis added.]

.   .   .   .

The cases above cited are those in which municipal corporations or
townships were incorporated into other municipal corporations or
political subdivisions. The following cases are those where the same
principles were applied as to school districts:

In Clother v. Maher, 15 Neb. 1, 16 N. W. 902, there were two
separate school districts, one of which had issued bonds. An act of
the Legislature consolidated these two districts into one under a
different name. The court held that, upon such consolidation, the new
district became invested with all the property rights of the two
constituent districts, and also became liable for the debts of those
districts, and that a tax for the amount of the bonded indebtedness of
the constituent districts was properly levied on all the taxable property
within the new district.

In Coler v. Coppin, 10 N. D. 86, 85 N. W. 988, it was held:

"A school township organized under chapter 44 of the Laws of 1883 became by such organization ipso facto liable for the debts of the old districts whose territory was included in such township."

In Abler v. School District of St. Joseph, 141 Mo. App. 189, 124 S. W. 564, it was held:

"Where one school district goes entirely out of existence by being annexed to or merged in another, if no arrangements are made respecting the property and liabilities of the district that ceases to exist, the subsisting district will be entitled to all the property and answerable for all the liabilities."

The above authorities are conclusive of the question under consideration. Upon the consolidation of the districts by the legislative act the entity of the districts as such was destroyed. So far as the fiscal authority of the constituent districts was concerned, that was absolutely destroyed by the consolidation. The result was, however, not that the debts were not still subsisting obligations, but that they became obligations of the consolidated district, which likewise succeeded to the property of the constituent districts. . . .

It follows, from what has been stated above, that the bonds voted are valid obligations of Parker school district, and that the permanent injunction asked for by plaintiff should be denied, and it is so ordered.

Guides for Class Discussion

1. Compare this case with *Board of Education of Barker District* v. *Board of Education of Valley District, supra* and *School District of City of Saginaw* v. *School District No. 6, infra.*
2. What line of reasoning did the court follow in arriving at its decision? Was this sound?
3. Is this decision equitable? Why or why not?
4. Do you think the court was right in applying the same rule to quasi-municipal corporations that it had applied to municipal corporations proper?

25. *"In the absence of a statute governing the situation, funds in the possession of a district from which territory is detached continue to belong to the district"* (p. 6).

SCHOOL DISTRICT OF CITY OF SAGINAW v. SCHOOL DISTRICT No. 6,
231 Mich. 664, 204 N. W. 737 (1925)
(Decided by the Supreme Court of Michigan)

[Plaintiff school district annexed a portion of defendant district. Later, when defendant received funds from the state representing its share of the primary school interest fund, based upon its enrollment before the annexation took place, plaintiff brought this action to recover its proportionate share of this amount, based upon the number of pupils residing in the territory annexed. The act under which annexation took place provided that any property situated in the annexed territory should become the property of the annexing district, which district should assume its proportionate share of the indebtedness of the district from which territory was taken.]

FELLOWS, J. . . .

•   •   •   •   •   •   •   •   •   •   •   •

By the plain language of this section upon the annexation of the portion of Buena Vista township to the city of Saginaw, that portion of defendant district so annexed to the city automatically becomes a part of plaintiff's district. . . . At the same time title to property "situated wholly upon the territory so annexed" passed to plaintiff, and it became liable for its statutory portion of defendant's indebtedness. The act, however, makes no provision for a division of the other property including uncollected taxes as did Act 141 of the same session, which applies to larger districts.

•   •   •   •   •   •   •   •   •   •   •   •

The trial judge denied plaintiff's right to recover on the authority of Township of Saginaw v. School District No. 1, 9 Mich. 541. . . .
In considering the question here involved, we should bear in mind that we are not considering a case of consolidation of districts where one district is wiped out. This annexation took but a part of defendant's territory, and left defendant an existing corporation with a portion of its territory intact. Cases of consolidation will therefore not be considered.

In Hampshire v. Franklin, 16 Mass. 76; it was said by Chief Justice Parker:

"By general principles of law, as well as by judicial construction of statutes, if a part of the territory and inhabitants of a town are separated from it, by annexation to another, or by the erection of a new corporation, the remaining part of the town, or the former corporation, retains all its property, powers, rights and privileges, and remains subject to all its obligations and duties; unless some express provision to the contrary should be made, by the act authorizing the separation."

· ·

The Supreme Court of the United States in Laramie County v. Albany County, 92 U. S. 307, 23 L. Ed. 552, thus stated the rule:

"Regulation upon the subject may be prescribed by the Legislature; but, if they omit to make any provision in that regard, the presumption must be that they did not consider that any legislation in the particular case was necessary. Where the Legislature does not prescribe any such regulations, the rule is that the old corporation owns all the public property within her new limits, and is responsible for all debts contracted by her before the act of separation was passed. Old debts, she must pay, without any claim for contribution; and the new subdivision has no claim to any portion of the public property except what falls within her boundaries, and to all that the old corporation has no claim."

· ·

While the Legislature has the unquestionable right in creating new school districts to transfer and provide for the transfer of the property of the old school district to the new district because it is public property . . . in the absence of express legislation on the subject the property of the old district except that in the annexed territory still remains its property unaffected by the annexation. Individuals and private corporations may be liable in an action for money had and received, where they hold money equitably belonging to another, but the rights, duties, and liabilities of public corporations which are the creatures of the Legislature are fixed by the Legislature. No act of the Legislature has been called to our attention, and we have found none, which changes the rule which is established by the authorities we have cited. We agree with the opinion of the trial judge in which he said:

"Upon the hearing of the argument the court was impressed with the equitable claim of the plaintiff and its right to recover. However, upon a careful examination and analysis of the statutes pertaining to the subject, the court finds no law giving to the city any right to make claim to any portion of this fund, notwithstanding the fact that it might be, and, in the opinion of the court is, as a matter of equity, entitled to the same."

The judgment must be affirmed.

Guides for Class Discussion

1. Compare this case with *Walker* v. *Bennett, supra.*
2. Do you think this decision is equitable? Give reasons.
3. Would the court have approved a statute that provided for an allocation of the funds in question?

26. *"School districts which have been illegally created may, nevertheless, function . . . as though they were legal . . . [if] they have attained the status of de facto districts"* (p. 6).

CLEMENT V. EVEREST,
29 Mich. 19 (1874)
(Decided by the Supreme Court of Michigan)

[This was an action to restrain the collection of school taxes, on the ground that the district levying them was without authority so to do. The court, overruling the lower court, issued the injunction prayed for against the board. It refused the defendant's right to challenge the legality of the district in this type of action. In rendering its decision the court found it necessary to comment on the legal authority of a *de facto* district.]

CAMPBELL, J. . . .

.   .   .   .

The bill in this cause was filed to restrain the collection of school taxes against the lands of complainants, levied on behalf of school district number three, in Pine Grove, on the ground that the township board of school inspectors had detached the lands in question from that district, and restored them to district number two, to which they had belonged before district number three was organized.

.   .   .   .

Two reasons are given for holding the change of districts void: *First,* that the inspectors were interested; and *second,* that they acted without proper notice.

There are some cases where the action of interested parties is forbidden by the principles of law. Public officers cannot contract with themselves as individuals, and cannot act judicially upon their own interests. They cannot usually occupy two conflicting relations.

But the interest which these officers had was that of taxpayers and residents, and the business they were engaged in was the public administrative business of their districts and township, in which no man could be found who was not interested in a similar way.

The degree of interest is not regarded in cases of disability. Any tangible interest prevails. If interest could prevent men from performing these local duties, they could not be performed at all. The policy of a republican government places all local interests in the hands of the electors most deeply concerned, and requires them to choose interested agents and representatives. The disabling doctrine has no application, and can have none, to those administrative acts which are public, and not with or between private parties. Such action is the action of the public, for itself and on its own behalf, and there are in law no conflicting interests which can be recognized as belonging to the individual representatives in the official body. We think this objection is unfounded.

We have referred to this point because it was very strenuously argued, and claimed to result from decisions heretofore made in certain cases involving interested action. . . . But we think there is an insuperable obstacle in the way of allowing any such objections. The board of inspectors act in the exercise of a public discretionary power in creating or changing districts, which can only be reviewed, if at all, by some direct appellate process which operates upon the proceedings themselves to affirm, reverse or change them. The subject is within their jurisdiction, and whether they have complied or not with all the directions of the statutes, that question cannot be examined collaterally. The present suit is not calculated to operate as an appeal, and is not brought by the public, or by any one authorized to seek a review in this form, inasmuch as this is not a suitable form, and is not appointed for that purpose. The attack comes from the defense, and not from the complaining party. Such a bill could not, by whomsoever filed, operate directly to affirm or annul the corporate action. If different suits were brought it might easily happen that the results would differ in the two, and the question could never be settled.

It would be dangerous and wrong to permit the existence of municipalities to depend on the result of private litigation. Irregularities are common and unavoidable in the organization of such bodies; and both law and policy require that they shall not be disturbed except by some direct process authorized by law, and then only for very grave reasons.

The policy of our law is to place the whole work of local administration in the hands of the people of the locality, and it cannot be expected that town officers will be always able to conform their actions to the strict rules of technical accuracy. In such matters as concern the public, and do not interfere with private property or liberty, such action as creates municipal bodies and gives them corporate existence cannot be questioned without creating serious disturbance. If the regularity of their organization can be kept open to question indefinitely, no one could ever be sure that any of the taxes or other matters concerning his own town were valid, and the whole public business might be blocked by litigation. There are some matters affecting private rights which are scrutinized strictly, because no one can be deprived of private rights without conformity to law. Where one man's property is taken for public purposes without his consent, the taking must be justified by regular action. But where the organization of a local corporation, as a town or district, is left to the will of any particular body of electors or officers, and they proceed to execute their powers and complete the organization, their executed will ought to stand if there has been a substantial compliance with the policy of the law giving them jurisdiction. Every presumption is to be made in favor of the regularity of such action; and where there is a valid law, and an organization under it which proceeds from the lawful agencies, it should be regarded as entitled to legal standing, unless measures are speedily taken to assail such action by some competent authority. Where an appeal is granted, it must be lawfully prosecuted. Where there is no appeal, the courts will never enlarge their remedies to interfere, where they can avoid it, with existing corporate bodies provided for by law, on any formal ground. The same rule which recognizes the rights of officers *de facto* recognizes corporations *de facto,* and this is necessary for public and private security. There are probably few towns or school districts where there has not been some looseness in proceedings to organize them. Such carelessness seldom leads to serious mischief, and where it does there are usually sufficient remedies without needless intermeddling. But the convenience and security of the vicinage cannot be left exposed to disturbance by every one who chooses to begin a law suit.

The district must be held legally changed. The decree below must be reversed, with costs of both courts, and a perpetual injunction awarded.

Guides for Class Discussion

1. Compare this case with *Coler* v. *Dwight School Township, infra* and *De Berg* v. *County Board of Education, infra.*
2. What line of reasoning motivated the court in arriving at its decision?
3. Do you agree with the court? Give reasons.
4. What does this decision add to your knowledge of the right of *de facto* districts to operate?

27. *"For a school district to be regarded as de facto three conditions must be met. . ." (p. 6).*

DE BERG V. COUNTY BOARD OF EDUCATION,
248 Iowa 1039, 82 N. W. (2d) 710 (1957)
(Decided by the Supreme Court of Iowa)

[Seven districts voted on a proposal to consolidate. In one district the proposal was rejected. In the other six it was adopted.
When an attempt was made to consolidate these six, which were
noncontiguous, its legality was challenged. It should be noted that
after an attempt was made to organize the six districts into a
consolidated district, an election was held in this newly organized
district and in the seventh to consolidate the two. The proposal
was adopted in both. The result was that all seven districts involved in the original proposal to consolidate ended up in the
same district.]

PETERSON, Justice.

. . . .

When the election as to consolidation failed, one of three situations
was present as to the six districts in question: (1) they were either
a de jure corporation, or (2) a de facto corporation, or (3) no
corporation.

We can quickly settle the first question. In accordance with our
recent decision of State ex rel. Warrington v. Community School District of St. Ansgar, Iowa, 78 N.W. 2d 86, they were not a de jure
corporation.

Was there a de facto corporation on which they could build a legal
consolidation? In the matter of business corporations we have defined
a de facto corporation in First Title & Securities Co. of Bloomington,
Ill. v. United States Gypsum Co., 211 Iowa 1019, 233 N.W. 137, 140,
73 A.L.R. 1196, as follows: "A de facto corporation exists so that
the legality of its subsistence cannot be attacked collaterally, where
(1) there is a special act or general law under which such a corporation
may lawfully live, [Emphasis ours] (2) a bona fide attempt to organize
under the law in colorable compliance with the statutory requirements,
and (3) actual user or exercise of corporate powers in pursuance of
such law and attempted organization." Supported by many citations.
Substantially the same definition appears in 13 Am. Jur., Corporations,
§ 49; and in 18 C.J.S. Corporations § 99. As a general principle this

definition is as effective in connection with school corporations as in the field of business.

We have not passed on the question directly as to school districts, but general law and decisions in other states support this position. . . . We quote from 78 C.J.S. Schools and School Districts, supra: ". . . where there is no law authorizing the creation of the district it cannot become a de facto district".

Referring to the elements of a de facto corporation as outlined in First Title & Securities Co. of Bloomington, Ill. v. United States Gypsum Co., supra, the first qualification for such a corporation is decisive of the question that defendants did not have a de facto corporation. There is no special act nor general law in the State of Iowa by which the type of organization remaining could "lawfully live", after the consolidation election failed. There is no judicial sanction for the existence of such a de facto corporation; judicial pronouncement is directly to the contrary in the St. Ansgar case.

In case of State ex rel. Consolidated Dist. No. 13, New Madrid County v. Smith, State Auditor, supra, (Missouri) there was an attempt to form a consolidated school district. The school district of town of Gideon contained 1233 children of school age in both the urban and rural areas of the town. On April 2, 1929 at the annual school meeting of the voters a proposition was carried to divide the district into a town district with 497 children of school age and a common school district in the rural area of 736 children of school age. Later in the month a special meeting of voters was called and on April 23, 1929, proposition was submitted and carried that the two districts which had been previously divided three weeks before, should be formed into a consolidated school district. The court held no legal consolidation was established stating as follows: "Thus it appears that the town school district of Gideon with 1,233 children of school age wanted to be a consolidated school district. However, the voters of said district were confronted with the Laws of 1925 . . . prohibiting the inclusion of a town district with 500 children of school age within the territory of a consolidated school district. In this situation they attempted to lay the foundation for the organization of a consolidated district by dividing the town district as above stated. There is no law authorizing the division of a town district, and the attempt to detach the 71 sections of land did not divide the district. [Five cases cited]. . . . It follows that the attempt to organize the town district into a consolidated school district was contrary to law and void. Laws of 1925, p. 330. Even so, relator contends that the district was a de facto consolidated district. We do not think so. There is no law authorizing said town district to incorporate as a consolidated district. Absent such a law, said district would not be a de facto district. In other words, there cannot be a valid de facto corporation, if there cannot be such a de jure corporation. . . . Furthermore, 'a de facto corporation can never be recognized in violation of a positive law.' Fletcher Cyc. Corporations, vol. VIII, p. 85."

During the interim, while the question of legality was being settled, the remnants of a district left after the unsuccessful consolidation election, could not be used as a lever to lift the district from illegality to legality. Defendants did not have a de facto corporation of such type that we can approve election of directors, legality, and merging with adjacent districts.

The third situation above stated became effective. There was no corporation in existence on which a merger or a new consolidation could be erected. Since one entity in the merger proceeding was not legal, it could not properly form the basis of a statutory consolidated school district.

Appellees in truth and fact claim to have a consolidated school district. It is a combination of seven previous districts, or parts of districts. Consolidated districts are fundamentally formed under Sections 275.11 et seq. If their claim should be approved the district was established by affirmative vote of six districts in May, and one district in August. This procedure we cannot approve.

.   .   .   .

The decree in this case dismissing plaintiffs' petition was filed on June 14, 1956. On July 26, 1956, we rendered and announced the decision in case of State ex rel. Warrington v. Community School District of St. Ansgar, supra. The principal question in the case was the identical question involved in this case. In the St. Ansgar case, after discussing the necessity of territory being contiguous in order to form a legal consolidated district under Section 275.11, we said: "The conclusion is unescapable that uniting territory into one contiguous body of land is basic in our present school reorganization legislation, that the language of the statute is mandatory and must be followed to establish a de jure school district." . . . We had previously decided in several cases that in order to form a valid school district, annexed, merged, or consolidated, areas involved must be contiguous. . . . We announced the doctrine in a decision written by Judge Ladd more than forty years ago in case of Smith v. Blairsburg, Independent School Dist., supra, where we said [179 Iowa 500, 159 N.W. 1028]: "A petition such as the statute requires need not follow any set form. All essential is that the boundaries of the proposed district be indicated, and *that the territory therein be contiguous.*" (Emphasis ours.) We have consistently supported this doctrine throughout the intervening years and as recently as 1956 in State ex rel. Warrington v. Community School District of St. Ansgar, supra.

Defendants used the six remaining areas of the proposed consolidated district as a basis for the creation of what they now call "The Community School District of Greene, Butler County, Iowa." They switched from the provisions of Section 275.11, which pertain to the consolidation of three or more districts, to the provisions of 275.10 which pertain to the merger of two districts. Under Section 275.10 there must be two legal districts involved in the process. This creates the difficulty involved in the present situation. In view of present day conditions in the Greene School District we would prefer to approve the status quo. However, we cannot approve violation of clear and specific provisions of statute for the sake of expediency. If we approve the ingenious method adopted in this area, it could easily become the basis for establishing numerous consolidated districts in the state, all established by judicial pronouncement instead of legislative enactment.

We have discussed the question of a *temporary* de facto corporation in connection with school or town corporations in three cases. In case of State ex rel. Cox v. Consolidated School District of Readlyn, supra, we considered the question incidentally. The proposed school consolidation had been declared illegal by the trial court in a quo warranto proceeding by reason of failure to properly publish notice. We affirm the decision. The trial court provided: "The decree provides further that since it is essential school facilities be maintained and since the school year commencing in the fall of 1953 is well advanced, the de facto corporation may continue to function 'until the end of the current year' ". In affirming the decision we approved this provision, but it will be noted that it is carefully restricted to a short and temporary period of time. In the per curiam supplement to opinion in State ex rel. Warrington v. Community School District of St. Ansgar, supra, we provided that the school district function as a de facto corporation during the school year 1956-1957, but also carefully provided that the district court take proper steps to dissolve the de facto corporation at the end of the school year. We made a similar provision in State ex rel. Mercer v. Town of Crestwood, Iowa, 80 N.W. 2d 489. These provisions can clearly be distinguished from any claim by defendants that they had a de facto corporation which could be used as one part of a program of merger.

Similar permission is in order in this case. In connection with remanding this case to the District Court of Butler County we provide that the court permit "The Community School District of Greene, Butler County, Iowa", to function as a de facto school corporation for the remainder of the school year of 1956-1957, or until with reasonable dispatch the necessary proceedings for consolidation can be taken in accordance with Sections 275.11 to 275.25 inclusive. After the de jure corporation has been established in accordance with provisions of statute the court shall take proper steps to dissolve the de facto corporation as of the end of the school year, if possible, but in any event not later than September 1, 1957.

Guides for Class Discussion

1. What three conditions must be met before the courts will recognize a *de facto* district?
2. What is a *de facto* district? A *de jure* district?
3. Do you agree with the court's decision? Give reasons.

4. Do you agree with that part of the decision that permitted the existence of a temporary *de facto* district until matters could be straightened out? Why or why not?

5. On what ground did the court permit the existence of the temporary *de facto* district?

28. ". . . *[the acts of a de facto district] are as binding as they would have been if the district had been legally created in the first place"* (p. 6).

COLER v. DWIGHT SCHOOL TOWNSHIP,
3 N.D. 249, 55 N.W. 587 (1893)
(Decided by the Supreme Court of North Dakota)

[This was an action on the interest coupons of certain school bonds. Defendant refused to pay the interest on the ground it had not issued them—the bonds had been issued by a local district which, later, became a part of the defendant district. Defendant contended that the local district should be held responsible for them. At the bottom of the matter was the question of the legal existence of the local district—District No. 22—at the time the bonds were issued. In respect to this matter the court considered the formation of the district and commented on the legality of acts performed by a *de facto* district.]

CORLISS, J.

. . . .

. . . A municipal corporation may have life, although there are no officers in office. No claim is made that the officers who in fact signed the bonds and coupons were not at least de facto officers of the district, provided there was a legal organization thereof. Nor could it be successfully contended that such officers were not at least de facto officers, there having been an attempt to comply with the law requiring the furnishing and filing of the description before officers should be elected, and the officers being in actual possession of their respective offices and exercising the function thereof, and there being no other persons pretending to lay claim to such offices. Nor would we reach a different conclusion were we of opinion that the organization of the district was so defective that the proceedings would be set aside on certiorari, or the right of the district to act as such would be denied by judgment in quo warranto. At the time these bonds were issued the district was acting as a de facto district under at least color of organization. It had elected its district officers; had held its district meetings; had voted to borrow money to build a schoolhouse; and it appears to be undisputed that the proceeds of these bonds were used for that purpose, and the inhabitants received the benefit thereof. A schoolhouse has been built, and school has been taught therein. To allow the defense that the proceedings in the organization were defective to defeat the debt represented by these bonds would, under these circumstances, be to sanction repudiation of an honest obligation. We are firm in the opinion that the legality of the organization of a municipal corporation cannot be thus collaterally attacked. Citizens of the district who are opposed to the formation of such a corporation are not without remedy. Certiorari will reach the action of the county superintendent when without jurisdiction. . . . The corporate existence may be attacked by quo warranto. . . . The evils resulting from a doctrine which would permit the legality of the organization of a municipal corporation to be inquired into collaterally—in an action to enforce a debt, in a proceeding to collect a tax levied by the de facto corporation, or in a litigation over a tax title growing out of a tax imposed by such municipality—would be as great as the evils which would flow from the collateral inquiry into the title of a person to an office, the functions of which he is in fact exercising. This same argument reaches the objection that no sufficient petition was ever presented and filed, even assuming that the record sustained the claim that this requirement of the statute was not compiled with. It does not follow, because the organization was illegal for want of power in the county superintendent, that at all times, in every species of litigation, and by any person, the existence of the de facto district can be assailed. It is no more essential to the exercise by the county superintendent of this power that a petition should be filed than that it should be signed by a majority of the citizens residing in the district. It is the fact, and not the decision of the superintendent that the fact exists, which gives him jurisdiction. A petition is filed lacking the signature of one citizen to make it a petition signed by a majority of the citizens; in all other respects the organization is regular; bonds are issued, a schoolhouse built, and school taught. Is all this to be ignored, to be treated as illegal, because there was no de jure district? Who are the real parties interested in defeating such a debt? The taxpayers within the district. In what position are those to object who participated in the organization? They have attempted to form a district. They for a time believe that they have formed it. They elect officers; borrow money on bonds for district purposes; build a schoolhouse therewith; and use the money for other purposes connected with the functions of the district. On what principle can the existence of the district be denied by them for their benefit? If any within the district refrained from affirmative action, still they are chargeable with passive acquiescence when they might have acted, and acted effectually, against the de facto existence of the district, and thus have prevented an imposition upon the innocent who were justified in taking that to be a legal district which was acting as such, and to all appearances was warranted in acting as such. Those who were silent, when in conscience they should have spoken, have no claim upon the equity of this court. They did not protest; they did not appeal; they did not resort to certiorari; they made no effort to have the district attorney overthrow this de facto district by quo warranto; and when the bonds were voted for they appealed to no chancellor to protect their property from an illegal debt. Not only the considerations which lie at the foundation of the rule protecting the public in dealing with a de facto officer, but also a principle very analogous to that of equitable estoppel, protects these bondholders against repudiation under the forms of the law. If there cannot be a de facto school district, there cannot be a de facto city. If illegality in the proceedings to effect organization is fatal to the existence of a district, it is equally as fatal to the existence of a municipal corporation of a higher grade. Given a case where the defects in the incorporation of the city are as fatal as in this case, and then deny to that corporation any effect although a city government is in fact inaugurated and carried on, and the consequences would be intolerable. Open and acknowledged anarchy would for some reasons be preferable. In after years tax titles would be destroyed; every officer of the city would be a trespasser when the discharge of what would be his duty on the theory of the existence of the corporation led to an interference with the property or persons of others. Every police or other peace officer and every magistrate acting under the supposed authority of the city government would be liable for extortion, for assault and battery, for false imprisonment, and could be prosecuted criminally for acts done in good faith in the enforcement of the criminal law. An army of creditors whose savings have gone into the city treasury, and through the treasury into public buildings and other public improvements, find, to their astonishment and dismay, that they have received in exchange beautifully lithographed but worthless bonds as souvenirs of their abused confidence. All that has been done in good faith under color of law is only barefaced usurpation, and to be treated as such for all purposes. Such a doctrine would be the author of confusion, injustice, and almost endless litigation. The imagination cannot embrace all the gross wrong to which it would lead when pushed, as it must be, to its logical consequences. On the other hand, no great injury can result to the citizens or state by recognizing a de facto corporation; one acting as such under color of organization. If the law is disregarded in the attempt to organize the municipality, the violation of law always can be nipped in the bud by appropriate judicial proceedings. We find that our views are by no means novel. The rule that the existence of a de facto municipal corporation cannot be collaterally assailed has frequently been recognized and applied by the courts. . . . In some of the cases time seems to have been considered an element of some importance, but the public may as effectually be deceived by a de facto organization the day after it is complete as a decade thereafter. The time a de facto officer has been in possession of an office is never regarded as controlling. He is as much an officer, as to the public, the day after he intrudes into the office as a year later. "The same rule which recognizes the rights of officers de facto, recognizes corporations de facto, and this is necessary for public and private security." Clement v. Everest, 29 Mich. 19-23.

Guides for Class Discussion

1. Compare this case with *Clement* v. *Everest, supra.*
2. Compare it with *De Berg* v. *County Board of Education, supra.*
3. Was the court's reasoning sound? Evaluate.
4. What did the court mean by the words "equitable estoppel"?

29. *"The law provides a special action [one in quo warranto] whereby the legality of a school district may be attacked" (p. 6).*

Spilker v. Bethel Special School District,
235 S.W. (2d) 78 (Mo.) (1950)
(Decided by the St. Louis Court of Appeals)

[Plaintiffs brought this action against the defendant district and the members of its school board to enjoin them from exercising any control over the money, property, and other assets of the "Brick District," on the ground that it was not legally annexed to defendant district, because of certain irregularities. Specifically, an attack was made on the legality of the annexation election. The lower court sustained the defendants' motion to dismiss the action, and the higher court affirmed the lower court's decision.]

Anderson, Presiding Judge.

. . . .

Defendants filed a motion to dismiss plaintiffs' petition on the ground that it failed to state a claim upon which relief could be granted, and on the further ground that plaintiffs did not have legal capacity to bring this action. The court sustained this motion and dismissed the case, and from the judgment of dismissal plaintiffs have appealed.

Plaintiffs' petition is as follows:

"Come now the plaintiffs herein and for their cause of action state:

. . . .

"(5) That after said election was held the results thereof were certified to the board of directors of the Bethel Special School District defendants herein; which board, by their order, accepted the Brick District.

"(6) Plaintiffs further state to the court that the election held in the Brick District was illegal and of no force or effect; that the defendants as members of the Board of Directors of the defendant Bethel Special School District are unlawfully attempting to take and assume control over all the money, property and other assets of the Brick District; that by reason of the election as aforesaid being unlawful and void the defendants have no legal right to assume any control over the aforesaid properties.

"(7) Plaintiffs further state that they have no adequate remedy at law, and that unless an injunction be granted against the defendants great and irreparable injury will be done plaintiffs.

"Wherefore, Plaintiffs pray the court for its proper order perpetually and permanently restraining and enjoining defendants from exercising any authority or control over the money, property and other assets of the Brick District."

Appellants contend that the trial court erred in sustaining defendants' motion to dismiss.

At the threshold of this case we meet this question: Can these plaintiffs draw into question the right of the Bethel Special School District to exercise its corporate powers within the territory known as the Brick District, which it claims to have lawfully annexed? We do not think so. It is our opinion that the facts alleged in the petition show a de facto annexation which can only be questioned by the proper State authority in a direct proceeding for that purpose. . . .

The . . . cases [cited] deal with the organization of consolidated school districts and hold that a private individual cannot attack the legality of the corporate existence of such school districts on account of any irregularity in their organization, but that such action can only be brought by the State in a quo warranto proceeding. The same principle should apply to a case such as the one at bar, where the legality of an annexation is attacked on account of some irregularity in the proceeding wherein the school district seeks to acquire additional territory. . . .

Some courts give as the reason for the above mentioned rule that corporate franchises are grants of sovereignty only, and, if the state acquiesces in their usurpation, individuals will not be heard to complain. Others base the rule upon consideration of public policy, emphasizing the importance of stability and certainty in such matters, and the serious consequences which might follow if the existence of a public corporation could be called in question by persons who do not have an interest in the matter separate and distinct from that of the State itself. But, whatever reason is advanced, the rule is unanimous that where a public body has, under color of authority, assumed to exercise the power of a public corporation of a kind recognized by law, the validity of its organization can only be challenged by the State. The same rule applies where such public corporation extends its authority, undercolor of law, over additional territory. Its de facto existence in such territory should not be allowed to be questioned by private individuals. . . . Such being the law, it necessarily follows that the trial court properly sustained the motion to dismiss.

The judgment appealed from is affirmed.

Guides for Class Discussion

1. Evaluate the reasons stated for the rule laid down by the court.
2. The courts frequently say that the legality of a district can only be questioned in a direct action brought for that purpose and not collaterally. What is meant by this?
3. Do you think the court's decision was sound? Give reasons.
4. Compare the decision with the one rendered in *Mesquite Independent School District* v. *Gross, supra.*

30. ". . . *if two districts claim the same territory, one may bring a direct action against the other challenging its legality, and need not resort to an action in quo warranto*" (p. 6).

WALKER REORGANIZED SCHOOL DISTRICT V. FLINT,
303 S.W. (2d) 200 (Mo.) (1957)
(Decided by the Kansas City Court of Appeals)

[This was an action brought by one school district against another district which had purported to annex a third district, to test the legality of the annexation. The first district claimed to be entitled to the third district by virtue of having taken the first valid step in instituting annexation proceedings. Before deciding which of the two districts was entitled to the third district, the court found it necessary to rule on whether an action in *quo warranto* was the appropriate action to test the legality of the district, or whether it could be done by a declaratory judgment action.]

HUNTER, Justice.

. . . .

It is well established that the legality of the organization of a school district cannot be inquired into by a suit brought directly by an individual, but must be assailed, if at all, by quo warranto in the name of the state through the prosecuting attorney or attorney general. . . . As stated in the Spiking case, . . . 245 S.W.2d loc. cit. 21: "In view of the facts alleged, a declaratory judgment action is not available to the individual plaintiffs who are residents, patrons and taxpayers of the reorganized district. . . . They are only indirectly affected by the lack of de jure existence of the reorganized district and the attempted action by them is in the nature of a collateral attack."

In Spilker v. Bethel Special School District, Mo. App., 235 S.W.2d 78, 80, it was held, "The same principle should apply to a case such as the one at bar, where the legality of an annexation is attacked on account of some irregularity in the proceeding wherein the school district seeks to acquire additional territory. State ex rel. Childs v. Board of Com'rs of Crow Wing County, 66 Minn. 519 [68 N.W. 767] 69 N.W. 925, [73 N.W. 631] 35 L.R.A. 745. Some courts give as the reason for the above mentioned rule that corporate franchises are grants of sovereignty only, and, if the state acquiesces in their usurpation, individuals will not be heard to complain. Others base the rule upon consideration of public policy, emphasizing the importance of stability and certainty in such matters, and the serious consequences which might follow if the existence of a public corporation could be called in question by persons who do not have an interest in the matter separate and distinct from that of the State itself. But, whatever reason is advanced, the rule is unanimous that where a public body has, under color of authority, assumed to exercise the power of a public corporation of a kind recognized by law, the validity of its organization can only be challenged by the State. The same rule applies where such public corporation extends it [*sic*] authority, under color of law, over additional territory. Its defacto [*sic*] existence in such territory should not be allowed to be questioned by private individuals. State ex rel. Childs v. Board of Com'rs of Crow Wing County, 66 Minn. 519, [68 N.W. 767] 69 N.W. 925, [73 N.W. 631] 35 L.R.A. 745."

However, a different question is presented here. Concededly, it is one of first impression in this state. Both plaintiff and intervenor are public school districts. Each in its public corporate capacity is claiming the same territory, the Coal Creek District. Each claims that this district is legally a part of its corporate territory. Each bases its claim thereto on the assertion that it was the one which took the first valid step to acquire the Coal Creek District. Both plaintiff and intervenor have a direct interest in the matter. There is no threat of harassment by individuals questioning the validity of a school district. To permit plaintiff and intervenor, in a declaratory judgment action, to determine the question of which took the first valid step to acquire the Coal Creek District does not appear to violate any of the reasons for the rule that an individual cannot question the legality of the organization of a school district by a declaratory judgment action, but must proceed, if at all, by quo warranto in the name of the State. Since the reason for that rule fails as applied to this case we do not apply the rule. We hold that a declaratory judgment action is an approximate remedy for the determination of the question of which of the two school districts took the first valid step to acquire the Coal Creek District. In so holding we note that the Supreme Court has been careful to leave the door open for the decision that the cases in which individuals are endeavoring to attack the validity of an annexation or a reorganization through a proceeding other than by quo warranto in the name of the State are not necessarily controlling where two school districts are claiming the same territory. . . .

Guides for Class Discussion

1. Compare this decision with *Spilker* v. *Bethel Special School District, supra.*

2. Is this an exception to the general rule relating to *quo warranto?*

3. Considering this case together with *Spilker* v. *Bethel Special School District, supra,* what is the general rule with respect to *quo warranto?*
4. How did the court justify its position?

Selected Bibliography

1. Edwards, Newton. *The Courts and the Public Schools,* rev. ed. Chicago: University of Chicago Press, 1955.
2. Garber, Lee O. *Yearbook of School Law.* "School District Reorganization." Danville, Illinois: The Interstate Printers and Publishers, Inc., annually since 1950.
3. Hamilton, Robert H. and Paul R. Mort. *The Law and Public Education,* rev. ed. Brooklyn: The Foundation Press, Inc., 1959.
4. Remmlein, Madaline Kinter. *School Law,* rev. ed. Danville, Illinois: The Interstate Printers and Publishers, Inc., 1962.
5. Reutter, E. Edmund, Jr. *Schools and the Law.* ("Legal Almanac Series," No. 17.) New York: Oceana Publications, Inc., 1960.